From Pain to Purpose

How I Came to Know God During a Season of Infidelity, Divorce, Debt, and Debilitating Thoughts

VERNELL DESLONDE

From Pain to Purpose: I Came to Know God During a Season of Infidelity, Divorce, Debt, and Debilitating Thoughts

Copyright © 2020 by Vernell Deslonde
Printed in the United States of America

EBook ISBN 978-0-578-75758-2
Hardcover ISBN 978-1-7357550-8-3

Visit the author's website at www.DrVernell.com

Edited by Candice L. Davis
Book design and cover photography by Brittney Murray

Unless otherwise indicated, all Scriptures taken from the Holy Bible, New International Version®, NIV®. Copyright © 1973, 1978, 1984, 2011 by Biblica, Inc.™ Used by permission of Zondervan. All rights reserved worldwide.

I have tried to recreate events and conversations from my memories to the best of my knowledge. Details in some anecdotes and stories have been changed or combined for ease of reading and/or to protect the identities of the persons involved. The names Isaac, Trinity, and Johnny are pseudonyms.

Although the author has made every effort to ensure that the information in this book was correct at press time, the author does not assume and hereby disclaim any liability to any party for any loss, damage, or disruption caused by errors or omissions, whether such errors or omissions result from negligence, accident, or any other cause.

This book is not intended as a substitute for counseling advice. The reader should consult a therapist in matters relating to his/her mental health.

Table of Contents

There is a time for everything,

and a season for every activity under the heavens:

a time to be born and a time to die,

a time to plant and a time to uproot,

a time to kill and a time to heal,

a time to tear down and a time to build,

a time to weep and a time to laugh,

a time to mourn and a time to dance,

a time to scatter stones and a time to gather them,

a time to embrace and a time to refrain from embracing,

a time to search and a time to give up,

a time to keep and a time to throw away,

7a time to tear and a time to mend,

a time to be silent and a time to speak,

a time to love and a time to hate,

a time for war and a time for peace.

Ecclesiastes 3:1-8

Introduction

Nearly ten years ago, I found myself in my darkest and most painful season. I'm not quite sure how I landed in such a desolate place, but there I was, in the middle of an unexpected and unwanted divorce. My world completely unraveled when my husband suddenly announced he wanted to leave our marriage. On that same day, I discovered he'd been involved in other intimate relationships during our marriage. Added to this, I was left with more than one million dollars in debt, two children, ages three and five, to care for, and no money in the bank or assets.

For years, I'd ignored the signs that my marriage was in trouble. I repeatedly overlooked his lies, suspected infidelity, and silent withdrawals. I thought, if I turned a blind eye to certain behaviors, our lives would inevitably get back on track. I was wrong. Imagine everything in your life falling apart all at once, your hopes and dreams collapsing with four words, "I want to leave." A divorce—with all that goes along with it—is a painful experience many people face, a nightmare in which you feel as if you're teetering on the brink of death without experiencing the finality death brings.

The end of my marriage and the weight of debt broke my resolve, shattered my confidence, and unearthed every insecurity and weakness I'd tried to hide over the years. I felt ashamed, exposed, and like I'd failed as a wife and mother. There were moments when I thought about giving up because I couldn't see myself rising above the unbearable heartache or gravity of my financial situation. I felt lost, defeated, and crushed. I could not believe how my life changed overnight. There were days and weeks when I begged and pleaded for reconciliation, only to be repeatedly turned down.

Everything in my life changed the moment I started to relentlessly pursue an intimate relationship with God. As I chased after Him and sought to be in His presence, I was led into what I can only describe as the most spiritually rewarding seasons of my life. God sustained, comforted, instructed, and most importantly, loved me through feelings of rejection, brokenness, and betrayal.

I didn't make it through my painful seasons because time passed, because I engaged in visualization or positive thinking, or because I sought help from a psychiatrist or psychologist, although some may find comfort pursuing those avenues. I didn't make it through because I received an apology or the closure I wanted either. My pursuit of the never-ending love of God held me together and brought me through. I received healing and comfort from the One who promised to heal the brokenhearted.

Despite my reluctant, irreverent, and inconsistent behavior as a believer in Christ over the years, He did not turn me away. Instead, He patiently waited for me to seek His face, kept His arms wide open to embrace me when I returned, and rejoiced when I decided to follow Him.

From Pain to Purpose isn't just a book about the sting of divorce, infidelity, and the ridiculous amount of debt I accumulated during my marriage, although I share these stories. This book is not about being rejected and abandoned. It's about Him and trusting Him to heal, deliver, and transform me amidst my pain and weaknesses and life's uncertainties. It is about regaining my connection with God, overcoming spiritual brokenness that came from wrong relational choices, awakening to God's intended purpose for my life, and becoming the woman He intended.

God first put it on my heart to write this book because He knows there are believers who don't know how to let Him heal, deliver, and transform them after they experience emotional pain stemming from infidelity, divorce, and rejection. I also wrote this book because I understand what it feels like to be cast aside after being rebuffed and to grapple with thoughts of failure, self-doubt, and battle with wrong mindsets related to dating and debt. I believe there are those who need to hear my story of how God helped me overcome pain, disappointment, fear, lack of confidence, insecurity, and chaos. Despite experiencing all these emotional injuries, God protected, corrected, and delivered me from destructive mindsets that once held me captive.

My affliction, which we all experience at different points in life to varying degrees, was never meant to destroy me. It was meant to teach me life-altering lessons about myself, develop my character, produce maturity, reveal my calling and purpose, and deepen my trust and obedience in God. The beauty of my seasons is that God intended them to be temporary and not cyclical.

This book contains biblical principles and insights on how to let God change your perspective on your situation and serves as a reminder of the importance of surrendering and trusting Him. Each chapter represents a season in my life and includes accounts of my personal story of how I came to know God more intimately. It took years of seeking God in Scripture and prayer, discerning His will for my life, hungering for His presence, humbling myself, and submitting to His will for me to uncover lessons that changed the trajectory of my life. Coming to know God and awakening to my purpose has been a process. It did not happen overnight, but occurred gradually, incompletely, and in some cases, incrementally.

Prayerfully, this book will shed light on questions that may plague you as you travel through seasons of life, such as:

∂ How can I trust again after experiencing rejection and betrayal?

∂ How can I forgive someone who hurt me?

∂ How can I overcome brokenness and become whole again?

∂ How do I reach my purpose?

I pray God will use my experiences to give you the answers to these questions and teach you how to be the best version of you that He created you to be. I'll walk you through the ways He transformed my life and taught me to become who He intended by restoring how I saw myself. I'll show you how I found fulfillment in my relationship with Him, uncovered and tapped into my God-given gifts, unlocked keys to financial peace, and began living driven by purpose.

As you read this book, my prayer is also that you find fulfillment and rediscover the many ways to know God more intimately. Whether you're single, married, or divorced, absolute dependence on God is essential to overcoming your pain and discovering your purpose. In the pages that follow, I will share with you, life lessons and offer you key thoughts revealed to me by God as I journeyed from a broken state to spiritual wholeness.

Knowing God
Takes time and effort
Means counting the cost
Necessitates faith
Involves trusting Him
Requires obedience
Reveals your calling and purpose

CHAPTER 1
Season of Disruptions

I have told you these things, so that in me you may have peace. In this world you will have trouble. But take heart! I have overcome the world.
(John 16:33)

BLISSFULNESS

There were two things I wanted most in the world as a young adult: to practice law and to marry the man of my dreams. I imagined a small but lucrative private practice, specializing in family or criminal law. The idea of a career in law and opening my own firm came from my desire to protect the legal interests and well-being of others. I saw myself wearing power suits and litigating cases on behalf of my clients in front of a courtroom filled with spectators. I pictured, by my side, a supportive husband, who would accompany me to various events. In my dreams, he was educated, well-dressed, astute, and handsome. He was physically fit, family-focused, and articulate. I pictured him captivating my heart with kind words and romantic gestures and sweeping me off my feet. Beyond his outward appearance and checklist of must-haves, I imagined someone who would see the real me as kind, loyal, lively, vibrant, and sharp.

I dreamt of us buying a large home with spectacular views, traveling the world, and staying in five-star resorts. I envisioned years of adventures and the quiet moments, just the two of us sitting next to each other while our kids slept and we contemplated how we'd spend our life together. I believed all these things and this person would make my life complete, blissful. But as the years went by, I wondered if the perfect man existed, so I focused all my attention on pursuing my dream of becoming a lawyer.

The day I received my acceptance letter to law school, I was overjoyed. Five years of working hard in college had finally paid off, and my dream of becoming a lawyer was within reach. Shortly thereafter, I packed all my belongings and moved from my beautiful beachfront college town in Santa Barbara to San Francisco. I felt so nervous but excited. Here I was, this young, black female, who grew up in a less than desirable neighborhood in Los Angeles, preparing to pursue my dream of starting my legal practice. I thought God had smiled upon me and my life was headed in the right direction.

By the end of my first year, I earned a spot on the dean's list for my outstanding performance and was offered a paid internship at Wells Fargo Bank in the litigation and real estate departments. The university had recently partnered with the bank to offer one deserving student the opportunity to learn the business side of practicing law. I was honored that the dean thought of me. I couldn't pass up such an amazing opportunity to intern in the legal field, something I'd dreamt of all my life. While the internship wasn't in the area of law I envisioned practicing, the experience would be valuable. So I jumped at the chance. I accepted the internship, and I could not believe my fortune.

The word excited can't encapsulate how I felt. I barely slept the night before my first day. I wanted to make sure I looked impressive. Remember Phylicia Rashad's character Claire Huxtable on *The Cosby Show*? She was sophisticated, bold, and strong-willed. She was elegant, intelligent, and street smart. That's how I saw myself. When I thought of what I wanted to wear on my first day, her classic style came to mind. I wore a simple, fitted navy blue skirt, matching blazer, and white silk camisole. To complete my look, I added navy blue pumps, sheer navy stockings, pearl earrings, and a necklace. I carried a black leather briefcase with my purse tucked inside. I made sure every hair of my Halle Berry hairstyle was in place. I was ready.

I parked my car a few blocks away from the building and walked down Mission Street with all the other business professionals headed to their offices. Passing by a storefront window, I caught a glimpse of how I looked in my power suit. I was pleased with the person I saw staring back at me. I looked strong, self-assured, and poised. I looked like Claire Huxtable.

Standing on the corner of Sutter Street in downtown San Francisco, I stared up at all the tall buildings. After taking everything in, I confidently walked into the building and made my way up the elevator. When I exited, a friendly face greeted me and directed me to wait for my mentor in the conference room. *A mentor*, I thought. This was already working out to be an amazing experience. My mentor, a tall, slim awkward man, walked into the conference room and excitedly greeted me, exchanged pleasantries, and then escorted me to my new office, where paperwork from the human resources department awaited my review and signature.

My corner office on the twentieth floor had amazing views of the city. After I settled in, my mentor introduced me to several attorneys and legal secretaries in the litigation department and then accompanied me to my meeting with the vice president. Everything was taking shape better than I could have imagined.

After working at Wells Fargo for a few weeks, I quickly realized I wasn't interested in staying for anything beyond the money. My monthly salary was $3500, more than enough to help pay my monthly expenses, but I felt bored and uninterested. The work was tedious. Granted, I was only an intern, so there was a lot of grunt work involved, but the reality of the internship was humdrum. I hated it!

I enjoyed dressing the part and pretending I was on my way to success, but something was missing. I felt lonely and unfulfilled. Attending law school had meant leaving my close friends, family, and social life behind. I had to start over. Even as someone many people considered an extrovert; my transition was difficult.

For years, I'd dreamt of becoming a lawyer, only to discover I didn't enjoy the process or the actual work. Initially, I thought I was bored because my internship wasn't in my areas of interest or because I missed home, but those were excuses. Deep down, I knew I didn't want to become a lawyer. But if not a lawyer, then what? In truth, I wasn't sure what I wanted to do with my life.

I wondered if I'd made a big fat mistake moving to the Bay Area instead of returning home to Los Angeles after I graduated from college. But to go home and leave everything behind would mean admitting I'd failed in some way. I was the first in my immediate family to attend and graduate from a four-year college and go on to graduate school. Everyone expected me to be successful, or maybe that's what I expected of myself. Either way, there was no way in the world I planned to go home without finishing what I started. Quitting law school, which amounted to failure, was not an option.

Rather than beat myself up over the thought that I might have made a mistake, I decided to put on my big girl panties and suck up the thought of defeat. I pretended to enjoy where I was in life and to believe I was headed in the right direction. For some reason, it was important for me to keep up the pretense. If anyone asked me how law school was, I enthusiastically replied, "It's great!" I never shared my doubts with anyone. I covered up my uncertainties. But each time I walked through those office doors and onto the elevator, my stomach tightened. My dream of becoming a lawyer was quickly fading.

On a day like many others, I was researching a legal statute when my mentor stopped me to introduce me to a recently hired paralegal who also attended law school. He had an athletic build and a beautiful smile. He wore brown slacks with an eggplant-colored, buttoned-down, long-sleeved shirt, a tie, and blazer. There was something magnetic about an attractive man wearing professional attire, and when I shook his hand, I smelled his Cool Water cologne. We exchanged greetings and chatted, and it didn't take long for me to observe that he was reserved, contemplative, and ambitious.

I was immediately drawn to his confidence. I watched as he walked into meetings as if he belonged there. He could easily have been mistaken for one of the attorneys because of how he commanded his audience when he spoke. He was a gifted communicator, verbally and in writing, and could eloquently and concisely express his viewpoint.

There was a gravitational pull between us when we were in the same room together. The energy felt magical. We often smiled at one another from across the room, and a few times, I saw him staring at me when he didn't know I was watching him from the corner of my eye. It was hard to focus on work when he was around. We spent hours closed in each other's offices, talking and getting to know one another. I'm surprised neither of us was fired.

As we chatted at work, during lunch, and outside of work, I noticed we were complete opposites. His father had been a professor at Stanford before he passed away, his mother taught microbiology at a local community college after she left medical school, and he was the grandson of a university president in the South. I, on the other hand, grew up in an urban, poor neighborhood in Los Angeles, attended public schools, where gang activity was prevalent, and was the product of two parents who worked hard to ensure I'd one day attend college.

Through our many conversations, I also learned he was adventurous and uninhibited, loved to drink and smoke, and enjoyed outdoor camping. I, on the other hand, was unadventurous and inhibited, did not smoke, and was a social drinker. I hated the idea of

15

camping because the very thought of insects gave me the heebie-jeebies. He loved skiing, and I hated cold weather. He liked trying new foods, whereas I stuck to basic seafood and American cuisine.

He talked about leaving family and friends behind to live abroad and wait tables at obscure restaurants, and I wanted to vacation abroad and preferred stable living. He loved playing soccer and basketball, working out at the gym, and reading literary works. I was an inactive couch potato who spent most of my free time watching television and reading urban fantasy books. He loved soft lighting and a quiet home, whereas I preferred every light on in the house and using the television as background noise. He listened to electronica, and I loved hip hop, pop, and R&B music.

Despite our differences, we were drawn to one another. Everything about him intrigued and intimidated me at the same time. He was polite, regal, and charming. He was unlike a lot of men I dated in my youth. That's not to say those men weren't generous or respectful, but I wouldn't describe them as polite gentlemen. They didn't run to open doors for me or walk around to the passenger door to open it and help me in and out of the car every time we went out. I didn't feel butterflies fluttering in my stomach when they reached for my hand the way I did with him either. They had other redeeming qualities, but those men couldn't compete with what this man possessed. He was mature, quiet, and reserved, which was how I saw myself and the opposite of how others described me.

In college, I had been negatively labeled because of where I grew up, the high school I attended, the way I dressed, and how I spoke. Jokingly, I was called "ghetto" and "hood." A student once said everyone knew when I walked into a room because my voice carried and I was noticeable. It wasn't meant as a compliment. I was accused of being uncaring, insensitive, and heartless by a few people I considered friends. Another friend described me as the Tin Man from *The Wizard of Oz* because they saw me as the girl without a heart.

When you grow up around violence and experience hardships, you can develop hardness in your character. You're more guarded and less inclined to let others get close. I truly wanted to let people get close, but I was too afraid and too emotionally wounded to let them in. But this man who captured my heart seemed to see the best in me.

He told me he was immediately attracted to me. He thought I was beautiful, confident, and bright. He commented on my ability to maintain my composure during stressful situations, noticed my warmth towards others, and praised my tenacity and resilience. He described me as like a gazelle because of my grace and quickness. His compliments were endless.

This was the first time anyone described me as I saw myself, even if my current self wasn't quite there yet. He saw the me I always wanted to be, the opposite of how others saw me, and my heart burst into a thousand songs. With him, I was a different me, more refined, better. I was becoming.

It's difficult to describe how this man captivated my inner being. He was unapologetic about who he was and inspired me to be the same way. In my mind, he was everything I wanted in a husband and more. My heart loved him before my brain could process what was happening. He was the man of my dreams.

FORWARD MOTION

By the end of my summer internship, we had grown closer. Our conversations and time we spent together increased and intensified. He continued to work at Wells Fargo, and I found a job as a receptionist during the day and went to law school at night. I finally shared with him my doubts about remaining in law school and becoming a lawyer, but he already knew about them. He told me that, each time he tried to discuss a case or statute, I quickly changed the subject. He smiled and said he knew I didn't want to pursue becoming a lawyer, but he'd been waiting for me to say it. He saw it. He saw me! No one else knew or saw it, but he did. There were times when I thought he could see right through me. I couldn't hide from him.

By the end of my second year, after my next paid summer internship at the State's public defender's office, where all of our clients were on death row, I made the difficult decision to leave law school, and I found my passion in the field of education. Counseling wasn't as lucrative as becoming a lawyer, but there was value in the work I chose. I wasn't bored. I was content with myself and in life. Likewise, the man of my dreams found his path. He completed law school and pursued a career in corporate employee relations.

Initially, it was difficult to accept the death of something I'd fantasized about since childhood, but I found comfort in having this wonderful man in my life. I even told a friend or two I thought he was sent by an angel. I wanted to believe he was God-sent because having him in my life made me feel like less of a failure after leaving law school and my dream of starting a firm. I convinced myself I'd taken the path to law school and gotten my internship so I could meet and marry him.

We dated for seven years. While that's a long time in dog years, it didn't always feel that way. When we met, I was still in my early twenties and not ready to get married. But in truth, if he'd asked me at the age of twenty-three to marry him, I probably would have jumped at the chance, whether I was ready or not. During that time, he took me to beautiful wineries, out for romantic dinners, and on weekend getaways. He showered me with gifts, loving words, and affection, and he was an incredible cook. There were times when we spent time together without talking, and we enjoyed the quiet and each other's company.

During our seventh year of dating, he finally proposed. I'd flown back from West Africa after a ten-day trip. Excited to see me, he picked me up from the airport and told me he wanted to take me out that evening. I wanted to tell him I was too tired, but I didn't have the strength to hurt his feelings. When I arrived home, I took a long nap, but I could have slept through the night.

When I awoke, he told me to wear something warm because it was cold outside. So I threw on a pair of jeans and a t-shirt and grabbed a heavy jacket. We drove to the Berkeley Marina, where we'd gone on our first date, to walk around. The winds were high, but luckily, my hair was braided, so I didn't have to worry about it flying in the air or slapping me in the face. We held hands as we walked along the pier, and then he suddenly stopped, told me he wanted to spend the rest of his life with me, got down on bended knee, and proposed. Behind tears and in front of onlookers, I said, "Yes!" At the same time, I thought, *When one dream dies, another begins*. My dream of marrying the man who stole my heart was coming to pass.

WEDDING DAY

Our wedding day was exactly the way I'd pictured, full of bliss. Our family and friends joined us to celebrate our union at a venue tucked away in the North Berkeley Hills with breathtaking views. The ceremony took place outdoors, overlooking the hillside. Our guests sat near the rustic cottage where the reception would immediately follow.

He wore a black, fitted tuxedo with a periwinkle cummerbund and bow tie, and his groomsmen surrounded him. I wore a low-cut, classic dress that abounded in lace. I'd never flipped through magazines and pictured myself in a certain type of wedding gown. I'd pictured myself married but not what I would wear for the ceremony. My preference for a wedding gown was more along the lines of elegant and simple and sleek to fit my small frame. I wanted satin instead of lace, perhaps something a modern-day Claire Huxtable would have worn.

The dress I wore was hand-picked by his mother and not something I would've chosen. But it seemed to make her happy. Truth

19

be told, I could have worn a sackcloth on my wedding day. All I cared about was marrying him.

He stood waiting for me under an archway adorned with flowers. After we exchanged our vows, he draped his arms warmly around my waist and delicately kissed me. Then, we turned to face our family and friends and jumped the broom. There was an eruption of cheers, thrown rice, and congratulatory remarks, and the party ensued.

My favorite part of the evening was our first dance. We were so happy. I pressed my face against his chest as he crisscrossed his arms around my waist, and it felt like he'd never let me go. There was safety in his arms. We danced through the night and rushed off to Hawaii the next morning for our honeymoon. I couldn't believe how my life turned out. I married someone who saw, accepted, and loved the real me.

AMBUSHED

After eight years married to the man I thought I'd grow old with and two kids together, he came home from an NBA game and announced he didn't want to remain in the marriage. I was devastated by his declaration and completely taken off guard. Phrases such as "I'm not happy" or "We're not compatible," are empty, meaningless, and vague. Those words failed to explain his decision to leave. It felt like I'd been abruptly fired from a job where I'd worked for years but was no longer considered a "good fit."

In my experience, there's no real explanation when you're no longer well-suited for a marriage, only the feeling of trying to figure out what the right fit might be. Instinctually, you believe an egregious mistake was made, and you remind your spouse of your proven track record, numerous contributions, and loyalty. On the receiving end, the message sounds like: "Thank you for your many years of love and service to the marriage; however, I've decided to move in a different

direction that aligns more with my vision for my life and core values."
You're left to speculate. "Is the decision performance related? Is there
someone else you plan to hire as my replacement?"

If you've ever been unexpectedly fired or prematurely released
from a marriage, you know it's crushing. You wonder if there was
anything else you could have done or said that would have made a
difference. You might expect a severance package for your dedicated
years of service and the impending loss of income, only to discover
that there's no severance package waiting for you.

When I pressed for the reason he wanted to terminate our
marriage, he simply said with an exhausted tone, "I don't want to do
this anymore." In disbelief, I asked, "Do what anymore?" His tone was
reprimanding and accusatory when he said, "This!"

Earlier that day, we'd argued about email exchanges I'd read
between him and some woman that suggested they were in a romantic
relationship, which he vehemently denied. I read several emails in
which she thanked him for taking her to the airport and making her a
CD with his favorite songs. It was clear from her messages that they
spent time together, and he later admitted meeting this woman at a bar,
but again denied being in an intimate relationship with her. He
expressed his belief that having female friends, women I never met,
was acceptable. He told me men and women could have platonic
relationships and those relationships were normal whether you were
married or not. When I expressed disagreement, which seemed to
further frustrate him, he suggested I was suspicious and insecure.

Amid tears, I'd asked, "Why? How could you do this?" He told
me he didn't have time to discuss my feelings because he was running
late for the Warriors game. I couldn't believe he chose to leave in the
middle of our conversation, but he did. When he left, I combed through
more of his emails and discovered exchanges with other women.

Admittedly, this wasn't our first conversation regarding alleged
infidelity, and in each case, he'd denied any relationships with other

women despite what I uncovered. Once, when our daughter was a toddler, I'd taken her to Los Angeles to visit my parents, and I couldn't reach him for the entire weekend. Later, he told me he'd gone with his best friend to the NASCAR races and was up late each night, which was his way of letting me know he was too busy to call. After I returned from Los Angeles, I discovered he'd spent the weekend with his ex-girlfriend from college and her friends.

On another occasion, he told me he was traveling to Las Vegas for the weekend with a male friend. While we dated, he'd expressed his dislike for going to Las Vegas, but when I asked him why he was going to a city he didn't like for recreational purposes, he stared at me. He had this way of telling me to back off without saying a word, and in the past, he'd told me my questions made him feel like he was being interrogated.

The entire weekend of his Vegas trip, I called and sent several text messages that went unanswered. When he arrived home, he smiled and lovingly said he was excited to see us, but he never provided an explanation for why he didn't return my messages. Other times, he simply disappeared to go camping alone. I no longer recognized the man who'd so quickly captured my heart. He'd gone from charming and respectful to disrespectful, dishonest, and secretive.

For years, I chose to accept his explanations or ignore his behavior, even when I suspected he was unfaithful, because I grew tired of confronting him and listening to his lies. So imagine my surprise when he came home and said he wanted to leave the marriage. I was completely blindsided. I thought, *Perhaps I pushed him too hard this time.* For a moment, I believed he wanted to leave because he was exhausted by my repeated phone calls to him after he arrived at the Warrior's game. And at that moment, I regretted forcing him to answer my questions about my suspicions of infidelity.

I hoped he was upset and just needed time to cool off. I didn't want him to leave the marriage and give up on years of togetherness or break apart our family. Our kids were ages three and five, and I wasn't sure how to explain to them his decision to leave. I heard myself suggest, out of desperation, that maybe he needed space and time away from me and the kids to think. I thought being married, having small children and a demanding job, and carrying insurmountable expenses was too much for him to manage.

I even suggested he get a hotel room every week to stay closer to work to alleviate stress and pressure. He poured so much time and energy into his career. He worked through the night on projects, left for work before the sun rose, and returned after the kids were asleep. I thought that if I made his life easier, he'd be willing to stay. A desperate part of me believed even an unfaithful relationship was worth sacrificing and fighting to maintain for the sake of the kids, financial stability, the longevity of the marriage, and love. There was something about me that, no matter how incompatible we were or how incomprehensible his behavior, wanted to hold on, to not give up.

I was an absolute mess. I sat on the couch, crying, trying to catch my breath. My eyes and mouth pleaded with him. I thought he would console me, but he stood his ground. He didn't reach for me in my anguish or vacillate. It was clear he'd made up his mind, not necessarily at that moment when he announced he wanted to leave the marriage, but perhaps months or years before he uttered the words.

Four years earlier, when I was pregnant with our son, my husband had suggested we see a marriage counselor. Perhaps this was when he began to feel our marriage was over in his heart. He said we needed to "discuss our inability to connect." I wondered how I could connect with someone who frequently ran away from life's demands, shut down communication, took time-outs from marriage and his family, and disappeared. His behavior and moods gave me whiplash. I didn't know why he wanted to go to marriage counseling, but it was clear we needed to meet with a trained professional to help us sort through dishonesty, frustration, and unmet expectations. I wanted to get to the root cause of our relational challenges. I hoped to discuss hurt emotions due to unfaithfulness and disappointment, so I went along with what he wanted.

Our lives had become busy, and I was swept up in working, parenting, and managing our household. Admittedly, most days, I was exhausted. We had an overactive and cantankerous toddler running around our home, and I thought that was why our interactions were filled with routine and no longer blissful. I also noticed he was emotionally distant at times and detached from our daughter and me. It seemed like he looked for opportunities to be away from us. As an introvert, I thought he needed more alone time and less noise.

THERAPY

He spent several days researching to find someone he believed had the pedigree, intellectual ability, and experience to deal with what he described as problems young couples face. After combing through the internet, he found someone he believed matched his criteria and suggested we move forward and schedule an appointment.

During our first counseling session, the counselor asked us both to tell her why we were there. *Finally*, I thought. I wanted to hear his perspective on why we needed marriage counseling.

He immediately jumped in and explained our challenge as our inability to connect as related to our interests and approaches to life, my insecurities related to other women, unmet expectations he had of me as a wife and partner, and my failure to follow through on promises, which resulted in imbalances. He further described my role in our marriage as a passenger, an observer and non-participant, while he did *all* the driving. He shared examples of taking on all financial burdens and decision-making in our relationship, and he suggested I wasn't carrying my weight and lacked initiative. He indicated he felt taken advantage of by me. Resentful and unhappy were words he used to describe how he felt in our marriage. After he laid out all the ways I was failing as a wife and partner, he ended by adding I was a good mother to our daughter.

If I didn't know better, I would have thought I was on trial for breaching my fiduciary duty as his wife. He nicely presented his interpretation of the facts and argument to the judge, our therapist, and sought an injunction to stop me from further causing damage to him. Once upon a time, there was an overflow of kind and loving words, romance, and compliments from him to me. It was hard to see how our life had become so complicated and filled with blame, frustration, and resentment.

When the therapist asked how I felt about his statements, I opened with an apology for how he felt and noted that his description of me was discouraging and disheartening. While it sounds strange to apologize to someone for their perception of you, I didn't want to mount a counterattack and try to prove he was wrong. Instead, I chose to acknowledge how he felt. Despite his disturbing depiction of me, I wanted him to know I tried so hard to be the wife he wanted and needed.

Interesting to me was that I couldn't recall him telling me what he wanted or needed in a wife. My interpretation of what I thought he wanted from me was based on what I saw growing up. My idea of a good wife was someone who nurtured, respected, and loved her husband. Likewise, I'd never described to him, during our dating season, the type of husband I wanted. I had shared that I wanted to marry him because of how much I loved, respected, and cherished our relationship. I suppose when you've been in a relationship with someone for a long time, you know what you like, dislike, want, and don't want. But do you tell your future husband or wife what you want and need in a marriage?

Nevertheless, after I shared my understanding of why we'd sought out marital counseling, I wanted to add a few thoughts. I believed our incompatibility and inability to connect were a smokescreen for larger issues. We'd dated for several years despite our dissimilarities and still chose to marry each other. And although we connected to one another on certain issues, we did not connect in the areas that mattered most to me, which were honesty, respect, and reliability as a father. I expressed my frustration of feeling like a single mother while he worked late every night and on Fridays went to hang out with friends while I cared for our daughter.

I also wanted to shed light on his comment that he took on all our financial burdens, which was true. There would always be an imbalance in what I could contribute because his job offered higher salaries, stock options, and bonuses each year, whereas my salary in education only came with a three-percent increase each year if I was lucky. Some years, the increase was one percent. I agreed, however, that he shouldered the bulk of our finances, not because he made more money, but because of our expensive lifestyle.

To illustrate my point, I shared an example of when my husband fell in love with a four-bedroom, two-and-a-half-bathroom house that he wanted us to buy in the Oakland Hills before our daughter was born. The house was built in 1930 and located in a wooded neighborhood with nearby grocery stores, great schools, and parks. It was close to freeways and was safe. One of the drawbacks of the home was that it had seventy-five stairs from the house to the garage, which sat at the top of the ridge. I knew our friends and older family members would have difficulty walking up and down the stairs to the house. I also knew that, at some point, we would want to start a family, and lugging children and groceries up and down seventy-five stairs would be a huge undertaking. When I expressed my lack of interest in the home as well as the higher mortgage payment and suggested we continue our search, he called me unsupportive, so I acquiesced.

He clearly wanted us to purchase the home. Before we closed on it, we lived in a luxury-style apartment and the rent was $1700 a

26

month. With the new house, the mortgage would be $5400 without homeowner's insurance, which was more than a $3700 a month increase. I thought we should remain in our apartment longer. However, my husband was insistent, so I stopped offering my input and decided to not disagree because it seemed to upset him.

Once we closed on the house, there was one large expense after the next. The sewage line backed up, which caused every toilet in the house to overflow and ruined the floors in the downstairs bathroom. The cost to unclog the sewage pipes was $5,000 plus an additional $2,000 to hire a plumber. Within the same year, there was an electrical outage with the lights that led from the house to the garage, which cost $4000. Without the lights, it was completely dark outside, and we had no way to see our way to the garage without a flashlight.

Because our home sat is a woodsy area, every raccoon, skunk, rat, tarantula, spider, and fly infiltrated our house. He knew of my fear of insects and distaste for wild animals, but he insisted on buying that home. I shared with the therapist how much I hated the house and that it wasn't worth the extra cost or aggravation to me. The therapist asked my husband if he knew I strongly disliked our home and didn't want to make the purchase, and he told her that, when he thought back, he recalled that I'd mentioned not liking the house. She asked him, "Then, why did you purchase it, knowing she didn't like it?" He told her that he was thinking long-term and not short.

Despite the financial imbalances, we lived in the house he chose for us against my wishes, he spent as much money on whatever car he wanted whether I agreed or not, and we vacationed where he decided. I explained that I let him make most of the decisions in our marriage because he no longer valued my input. If I disagreed with his position, he seemed frustrated, so I stopped disagreeing and no longer took initiative outside of my expected role to agree with his decisions. It sounds like I was being passive-aggressive or even petty, but I was mostly frustrated.

My husband's appetite for purchasing things only increased. No matter what house we lived in, the car we drove, or the money we had, it was never enough. He wanted us to move into a bigger home with a higher price tag and drive more expensive cars every three years. I couldn't keep up with the things he desired in life and be expected to equally contribute.

After the words tumbled out of my mouth, I realized that I too felt resentful. I resented the decisions he made for our family without my input. I hated that he no longer valued my opinion. I detested his behavior. I loathed the person I'd become, weak and dependent. I disliked how he saw me and how I saw myself.

During another session, we talked about my husband having female friends who I'd never met. I could tell he was bothered when the therapist asked him to explain his thought process and why would he continued certain behavior that upset me. He stood his ground and held to his belief that having those female friends was acceptable, and again, he denied being unfaithful.

Each night after we left our sessions, he seemed more bothered and frustrated. He began making negative comments about our therapist. He thought she was biased and failed to help us deal with our challenges. He also commented that her $125 per session fee was too expensive for her services.

After a couple of months, my husband decided he didn't want to return to counseling. He said that our therapist seemed more sympathetic to me because I was a woman, and she couldn't understand his viewpoint. I reminded him that he chose her. What I believe prompted his decision to end our sessions was when our therapist mentioned that she wasn't sure why we needed counseling because we seemed to connect, still laughed together, maintained physical touch, and remained open to listening to each other. She said we needed to be more accommodating towards one another and learn to compromise more and suggested to him that it was important that he not bully me into submission even when he believed his decision would benefit our family. She told me I needed to find my voice and stop agreeing with decisions when my opinion differed from his. He disagreed with her assessment.

Our therapist noted that conflict avoidance was prevalent in our marriage. She pointed out that I suppressed my emotions because I did not want to upset my husband, so I often avoided conflict. She told me it wasn't good to suppress my emotions because they would inevitably explode, which is what happened when I confronted my husband about the email exchanges.

Somewhere along the way, I'd stopped expressing how I felt. Interestingly, I was raised to embrace conflict, to nip things in the bud and not to let hurt feelings and anger linger. It was normal in my household to prove my point loudly and strike down opposing arguments. Growing up, I dealt with conflict combatively, with anger, and defensively. It didn't start that way, but later in marriage, I avoided conflict.

In the early stages of our relationship, I frequently expressed what I thought and felt. Perhaps too much and, at times, explosively. Over time, I noticed how uncomfortable it made him, so I simply stopped engaging in matters that caused conflict to avoid pushing him away. I chose to quiet my voice. I changed to fit who I believed he wanted or needed me to be. I cannot cast blame on him for the choices I made. I'd expected marriage would bring me wedded bliss, my version of happily ever after, only to discover my fantasy was exactly that, fantasy. I found myself trying to conform and change to fit what I thought that my husband wanted. I barely recognized myself.

Life Lesson #1
You will not need to act differently to please the person God has for you.

Avoidance was a symptom of a larger communication problem in our marriage that went unaddressed for years. I underestimated the importance of addressing his pervasive patterns of behavior or my struggles that jeopardized my emotional well-being. Perhaps my husband's description of me as a passenger in the relationship was accurate. Maybe I wasn't present in the ways he needed.

Two years later, he decided to seek private counseling sessions, this time with a male therapist. He told me he was unhappy and thought he was depressed. When the therapist told him he was not clinically depressed, he blamed me and our life together for his unhappy state. He suggested he wanted more from life and I was holding him back.

I tried everything I could think of to make him feel happy about me, our children, and our life. While I knew that it wasn't my job to make him happy, it didn't prevent me from trying. I wanted to fix our marriage. I practically twisted myself inside out, trying to fix my faults and flaws. At the time, I couldn't see that my marriage was over. I was blinded by how I felt. We had some bumps and boulders in our path that I thought were movable, but if I'm being honest, I didn't want to see them. The Lord could have dispatched a legion of angels to tell me my relationship was over and it was time to move on, but I would have likely continued fighting in vain. Neither of us was perfect in our roles as husband and wife, but I was convinced that our marriage could be saved. Again, failure was not an option. I'd already let my dream of becoming a lawyer slip through my fingers for good reason, despite finding a better path, but I couldn't accept that my marriage had failed.

Life Lesson #2
You can only see what you are willing to see.

WARNING SIGNS

Looking back, there were multiple signs that my marriage was crumbling, some subtle and others glaring. I ignored those obvious signs, such as my husband working late most nights, emotional distance, avoidance, his unfamiliar female friends, not answering calls from his female friends while I was with him, and disappearing for long weekends without calling.

While we'd dated, he was determined to move up the career ladder. He worked hard and put in long hours to advance his career. Initially, I thought his ambition, drive, and determination were admirable. Those qualities were part of why I was attracted to him, but once we started our own family, I thought he would make concessions. Instead, he continued to work long hours and spent less time with me and the children. The more he focused on work, the more he became distant. He was changing. Our kids repeatedly asked me if he still lived with us or not. Each time, I jokingly responded, "Of course he does."

The glaring signs included his late-night work schedule. He left early in the morning before the kids were awake and came home after they were tucked in. One night, he pulled into the driveway, while talking on the phone, at 2:00 in the morning. I noticed from the front door that he sat in his car to chat on the phone for a while. When he continued to stay on the phone, I met him at the car to greet him. I had to tap on the window to get him to roll it down although he saw me standing there, and he immediately became angry. I asked who he was speaking with at that hour, assuming it was his best friend, and he told me to stop asking him so many questions.

He also stopped wearing his wedding ring. When I asked him why, he told me he'd injured his finger playing basketball and the ring became uncomfortable. I suggested we get him another ring to wear, which he chose not to do.

> ### *Life Lesson #3*
> *Don't turn a blind eye to signs that the relationship is in trouble or over.*

But why did I want to stay in a marriage that had fallen apart? The truth was I didn't have the emotional and mental strength to walk away. Relationships can be emotionally and mentally taxing, and rational thought doesn't always come into play. I was exhausted and depleted by the ongoing demands of motherhood, being a wife, dealing with debt overload, and juggling my career. I could not take on the task of confronting my husband about his checkered lifestyle and lies, make big decisions about the welfare of my children, and pack up to leave my marriage. I was overwhelmed.

The other reason I chose to stay was because of my pride. I'd invested so much time and energy into our relationship and wanted to see a return on my investment. I'd devoted countless hours, forgiveness, and love that I hoped would pay off in the end. However, our relationship had negative equity. My investment of time and energy was worthless. My pride left me vulnerable, broken, and in a perpetual state of compromise.

Another reason I stayed was because I was raised to endure. I was indirectly taught from an early age to stay in a marriage "for better or worse." Quitting wasn't in my DNA. I'd watched my parent's travail through "better or worse" situations without giving up on one another. I'm sure there were times when they wanted to quit, but they stayed. I knew my husband and I were in a rough season, but I didn't consider that the marriage could be over. Admittedly, we both had many idiosyncrasies and unaddressed issues, stemming from childhood, that negatively impacted our marriage. While our relationship wasn't perfect, I never imagined divorce would come to my doorstep. But there it was, taunting me.

CHAPTER 2
Season of Emotional Affliction

When I am afraid, I put my trust in you.
(Psalm 56:3)

DECISIONS, DECISIONS, DECISIONS

There were so many decisions I needed to make after my husband's bombshell announcement. But at the time, I couldn't think clearly. I barely had time to process what was happening. I was uncertain about what lay ahead for my children and me. It's not like there's a manual that outlines what to do after your spouse declares they're finished being a husband or wife. Perhaps some type of practical guide exists, but I was at an absolute loss. My thoughts were consumed with the present moment. I wondered if he would pack a bag and go to some undisclosed location or stay in our home and stare at me while I cried.

Living in the same home with someone after they say they want to leave is awkward. In the movies, the spouse who wants to leave dramatically throws his or her clothes in a bag, declares they'll return for their things later, and walks out of the house with the other spouse standing in disbelief. That didn't happen, and I didn't understand the rules of engagement or what to expect. If my husband had said he wanted to separate temporarily, we could have discussed the length of time and other pertinent information. But he simply said, "I want to leave our marriage" and "I don't want to do this!"

There were so many questions I wanted to ask him. *Where do you plan to live? How often do you want to visit the children? How should we manage our finances moving forward?* The list went on. Yet, I didn't ask any of those questions. My thoughts were disorganized because I was still in shock. After all my crying and sniffling subsided, we got dressed for bed and lay with our backs to one another.

Within in a week or so, I packed a bag and drove to my parents' house in southern California as my husband traveled to Seattle for work. I could barely stand to be in the same house with him because of the deafening silence. He no longer engaged in small talk or shared his day with me. He just walked through the door, went into his office, and ignored me. I felt the urge to escape his indifference.

When I arrived in southern California, I didn't immediately tell my parents what was happening. I just wanted to spend time with my kids, who I would leave with my parents for the summer. I called my husband several times while he was in Seattle, trying to reach out to plead my case again, and he sternly told me, "Stop calling me!" It was as if I was in the Twilight Zone. Who was this person who sounded like my husband, but was cold, firm, and detached? It was the first time I could recall him ever raising his voice. Granted, we'd had our disagreements over the years, but I considered him too much of a gentleman to curse or raise his voice above a normal tone. There was finality in his words. Afterwards, I had a stabbing pain in my chest, laced with denial, regret, and unimaginable agony. I wondered when he started to despise me.

I spoke to my best friend, Dayshawnna during my visit and I told her what my husband said. Needless to say, she was upset and shocked by his behavior. In all the years she'd known me, this was the first time she ever heard me cry, which pained her. She grieved with me through

34

my separation. There were times when she cried because I didn't have any tears left. Whatever ounce of strength I had disappeared that day.

She encouraged me to share everything with my parents. I was reluctant, but mainly embarrassed. My parents were married for more than forty years. I'm pretty sure at some point in their marriage they were unhappy. They may have even resented each other over the years. But they chose to stick it out. Because of this, I was afraid they wouldn't understand. Frankly, I didn't understand what was happening. I thought I would eventually tell them everything once I could do so without crying my eyeballs out.

When I decided to share with them what was happening in my marriage, I had to push aside all my fears, insecurities, and the idea that, yet again, I'd failed. My father was out running errands, and I was in the house with my mother while my kids slept upstairs. Before I knew it, the words tumbled from my lips. My mother was shocked. Understandably, she had so many questions. She was concerned about where we would live and our safety.

The idea of being a single mother of two children under the age of six scared me. I'd heard so many horror stories on television about abductions, and I was a nervous wreck. My mother, on the other hand, was seemingly calm.

When my father arrived home, he walked into the family room and saw me crying. He stood there, watching me, and waited for someone to tell him what had happened. Suddenly, my mother burst into tears and told him. I suppose she felt she could be vulnerable now that my father was there. He looked sad, disappointed, and angry. Whatever respect he had for my husband ended that day. My father asked why he wanted to leave, and I told him my truth. "I do not know."

When you try to explain to someone why a marriage ended, it's difficult to put into words. It's hard to provide an explanation people can understand, particularly when you're uncertain. I left out all the details about his infidelity, probably because they were irrelevant. But I felt relieved once I told my parents, and they were incredibly supportive.

After I dried my eyes and attempted to remove any evidence that I'd been crying, I went upstairs to spend time with my children. Later that day, I told them we were going to be moving into our own place. Fortunately, my children didn't have a clue what it all meant. I told them the three of us were going to find a new home to live in and daddy would find himself another home. I told them with such enthusiasm that they cheered. They smiled and gave me a hug.

I decided to take time off, and I called my office and made up an excuse for not returning. My office allowed me to use several sick and vacation days, and the remaining time, I worked remotely. I needed time to think and recover. The next day, I went into my mother's office and looked for rentals outside of the city where we resided. For obvious reasons, I wanted to create a physical distance between my husband and us.

After two weeks, I decided it was time to return to our house, start packing, and find a place to live. I felt an incredible amount of dread. I did not want to face the man who no longer wanted to speak with me. I was angry about how he'd treated me and embarrassed. Somehow, my desire to speak with him made me feel like a nuisance, which looking back, was likely true, but I could not reconcile in my heart his harsh words.

When I returned, I felt relieved when I didn't see his car in the driveway. Given the time of day, I'd assumed he wouldn't be home from work yet. In the past, I would have called to let him know I was returning, so he could help with my luggage, but I did not call or text, per his wishes.

When I walked through the door and made my way inside, I noticed all of his belongings were still there. Initially, I was confused. From his tone, I'd expected to return to an empty house. I also assumed that, if he did move out, he wouldn't tell me where he lived. I had an entire monologue in my mind of feelings I wanted to express and other things I wanted to say when I saw him again, but the sound of someone opening the front door, after three hours, interrupted my thoughts.

Our home had three levels. On the first level were his office, the laundry room, living and dining room, kitchen, and deck. On the second level were the master suite, my office, my son's room, and two bathrooms, and the third level were my daughter's bedroom and bathroom. I heard his footsteps on the hardwood floor of the first level of the house. He knew that I was home because my car was parked in the driveway. After five minutes or so, I heard him walk down the stairs towards our bedroom.

He opened the bedroom door and had a huge grin on his face. "You're back!" I was utterly confused by his excitement. One minute, he angrily told me to stop calling him, and the next, he was seemingly happy that I was back home. Normally, I would have raced to him to embrace him and kiss his cheek, but I stood in place, perhaps with a look of shock on my face. For the first time in weeks, he seemed like his former self, lively.

He told me he'd made reservations for a weekend getaway at a beachfront hotel in Santa Cruz for the two of us. It would have been the perfect time for me to throw everything back in his face or even ask him if he'd loss his mind. Instead, I listened and nodded. I was at a loss for words. Despite his sharp words two weeks earlier, I wondered if he felt remorseful and wanted to reconcile, but I was reluctant to go and afraid that the dark side of his Jekyll-and-Hyde persona could emerge at any moment. But I went because I was curious and hopeful that he'd changed his mind.

The following weekend, we drove to Santa Cruz. The drive was quiet, which didn't bother me as much as his silence. After we checked into the hotel, we looked for a place to eat and decided to dine at the hotel restaurant which had low lighting and a picturesque view of the beach. Everything about our dining experience seemed very romantic, but it wasn't. The ambiance was perfect, but he was stiff and distant again. At first, I thought that he was feeding off my aloofness, but as I suspected, his alter ego had returned. Rather than try to make a connection, I waited for him to engage in small talk and build up to why he wanted to end our marriage or declare regret. But we barely spoke to one another. The entire weekend, we silently walked along the beach, visited shops, and dined at nice restaurants. We sat down on the cold sand and stared out into the water without uttering a word to each other.

It was the most bizarre experience I've ever lived through. My husband, who'd said he wanted to end our marriage and told me to stop calling him, decided to take me on a romantic getaway. Only to get there and spend the entire weekend with few words exchanged between us. Imagine that. In hindsight, I believe the trip was his way of saying goodbye and good riddance, which I found annoyingly insulting and confusing.

BUSINESS AS USUAL

When we returned home from Santa Cruz, it was business as usual, living in the same house and living separate lives. We walked around our home like virtual strangers. He no longer told me when he was leaving the house or when he planned to return, and I wondered if he'd come through the doors every night. He didn't discuss with me his plans for moving forward, only that he no longer wanted to do "this." Everything felt so abrupt and final. I suppose, once he'd made his intentions known, he no longer felt obligated to engage with me as if he were my husband.

After dealing with his indifference for several days, I reviewed the list of rental properties I'd made when I was at my parents' house. I chose to look for properties in a city thirty-five miles from where we lived, not just because of the distance but also because of the beautiful lake and parks. I wanted to rent a two or three-bedroom apartment, but I soon grew tired of looking.

On the phone with one of my sorority sisters while I was out searching for a place to live, I told her how mentally exhausted I was from all my emotions. I told her I wanted to go home and rest, but she encouraged me to keep looking. I knew she was right. There was no point delaying moving out. After I drove around for several minutes, I stopped at the last place on my list. It was exactly what I was looking for.

When I returned home, out of habit, I attempted to have my husband weigh in on where the kids and I would live, but he showed little interest. I'm not sure why I tortured myself by sharing my plans for moving forward. There was a part of me that wanted him to insinuate himself. It would have been a sign that he cared. But the truth was again staring me in the face. He. Did. Not. Care. Where. I. Lived. He only seemed to care about when the children and I were moving out. So that's what I did. I moved out with practically no money in the bank while he sat in his home office, surfing the internet, and never even saying goodbye.

I must admit moving out of my home hadn't been my idea. I'd considered staying while he found another place to live even though I knew I couldn't afford the mortgage on my own. I wasn't certain if he would help me pay the mortgage, and if he did, I didn't know for what length of time I'd have his help. Given his past behavior and mood shifts, I decided it was best to leave, but I'd delayed leaving for several weeks.

During this time, a trusted friend and woman of God, who I knew had a strong prayer life, gave me two prophetic words she received from the Lord. First, she told me that the Lord wanted me to leave my home quickly. In retrospect, I believe God knew if I stayed, I'd continue to live in a perpetual state of compromise, allowing my husband to mistreat me and disrespect our vows all because I wanted to remain in the marriage.

There are times when God shows us that we need to move forward, but we delay leaving. This was the case with Lot who hesitated when the angel of the Lord told him to quickly leave Sodom because God was going to destroy the city (Genesis 19:15). Scripture points out that Lot lingered (Genesis 19:16). Perhaps Lot lingered because he didn't want to leave what he loved behind, like I lingered in my marriage despite the signs that it had run its course. I did not want to leave behind the person I loved and the life we built together.

Life Lesson #4
Do not linger when God calls you to move quickly.

As difficult as it was, I did exactly what she said. I left quickly, and to this very day, I'm so thankful I listened. The reality was that I didn't want to stay in a house we'd shared and watch him pack up and leave. I couldn't bear the thought of him stopping by to visit the children and then walking out, leaving our lives, over and over. I didn't want to drown in a sea of matrimonial memories either. Every room in our house reminded me of him.

Second, the Lord told her a woman who worked with my husband was encouraging him to leave me and our children. If I wanted to know who the woman was, then I should go to his office. Given his pattern of what looked like infidelity, the possibility that he was romantically involved with someone at work didn't surprise me, especially considering that was how we met. When I asked my husband if he'd shared our marital challenges with someone from his office, he denied it.

Before we separated, he'd often shared stories of a woman at work who he said he mentored. He assured me his relationship with her was completely platonic. I later discovered, right before I moved out, that he was romantically involved with her. I found movie ticket receipts from his email for two, for a movie I never saw, and Open Table reservations for two that he sent to his mentee's email address. It was clear he dated other women soon after I moved out of our home, and it was clear he had seen other women during our marriage. I didn't think there were any shards of my heart left to break. I racked my mind with the question "How did we get here?" My life wasn't what I'd expected or dreamed it would be.

CHAPTER 3
Season of Regained Connection

In my distress I called to the Lord.
(Psalm 18:6)

GOD HELP ME

After my marriage imploded, I was grief-stricken and broken. Not the type of brokenness that naturally heal overtime or is quickly repaired, but the type that forcibly and perpetually brings you to your knees from anguish. I didn't know how to move forward without the man who I started dating in my early twenties. The one who saw me. My entire life was wrapped up in him.

I went to work every day and put on a brave face, pretending all was well in life. I didn't tell many of my friends what was happening. I was humiliated that my husband had left, and I was afraid someone would find out and expose my secret. I carried so much shame and chose to isolate myself for two years. Who wants to admit their marriage unexpectedly ended? The first question someone would likely ask is, "what happened?"

To avoid embarrassment, I stopped attending various functions, didn't post on social media, and seldom answered calls. If I ran into someone who knew me, and they asked how my husband and the kids were, I smiled and enthusiastically said, "They're fine." But I was far from fine. I thought I was on the verge of suffering a nervous breakdown. I could not find rest for my mind or soul. Most days, I felt nauseous, like my stomach was twisted into a million knots. I needed answers for my grief that my husband did not or could not provide, so I sought out the One I knew had all the answers.

I was raised and baptized in church and taught that God was the answer to all life's problems. If I was upset, concerned, afraid, hurt, or worried, I was instructed by other believers to trust God. If I needed comfort and relief when life became too difficult, I was advised to pray. Well, everything in my life had turned upside down and I needed God. The stress and anxiety were overwhelming. I thought I would collapse from trying to manage my sinking emotions and care for my children at the same time. Feelings of abandonment, rejection, not being good enough, and sadness engulfed me. I was desperate for God's help, but I didn't know how to reach Him. I was unsure how to interact with someone who I hadn't spoken to in more than a decade.

I had a problem. While I believed in God, I didn't know Him. I confessed, accepted, and believed by faith in the resurrected Jesus Christ and understood that He is the road to salvation. I believed and still believe in God the Father, the Son, and the Holy Spirit. At the time, believing in God simply meant I believed He sent his Son from heaven to die for my sins, but belief in God is only part of the Christian walk. Even demons believe in God and shudder in fear (James 2:19).

I didn't understand the power of moving beyond belief to knowing Him deeply. For years, I thought I knew God because I believed in Him, had knowledge of Him, and went through the religious motions of attending church, kneeling down in prayer, taking communion, dropping money in the collection tray, and singing hymns. I sat in the pew, bowed my head, and nodded on cue when the pastor shouted. I recited the Lord's Prayer and said quick prayers over my food. I uttered spiritual clichés, like "God is good," "Thank you, Jesus," and "What a blessing!" to name a few. Yet, all these motions and platitudes were empty.

Consider when Jesus told the woman at the well that the Samaritans worshiped God but did not know Him (John 4:22). Think about when He told religious leaders that knowing scripture did not mean they knew God (John 5:39-40). Similarly, although I went to church, lip-synced hymns alongside other worshipers, and occasionally thanked God when life went the way I wanted, none of it meant I knew Him.

Admittedly, knowing God and developing a relationship with Him beyond my empty religious expressions hadn't been a priority. I became so entangled in life's demands, expectations, busyness, and self-serving behaviors that it didn't occur to me to seek to be in His presence until my life took an unexpected nose-dive and all my hopes and dreams went up in flames.

One night, I was on the phone with my best friend, Dayshawnna expressing my disbelief and fears related to my husband's desire to leave our marriage and the idea of raising our children on my own. I'm sure she heard the despair and devastation in my voice. She listened as I replayed the last fifteen years of my life. She knew how helpless and empty I felt, and she prayed and asked God to strengthen me, bring me comfort, guard my heart, and to restore my marriage because she knew I wanted my husband to return. When she prayed, I thought the angels in Heaven were encamped around her because I felt this unexplainable sensation of peace surround me. There was power, authority, and reverence, in her voice. And each time that she prayed with me, over a period of several weeks, my sorrow went away, and I didn't feel the sting of abandonment and rejection.

It was the first time in my life that anyone ever prayed out loud for me. I knew my mother prayed for me, but she did so silently during her time with God. What I needed most was someone to intercede with God on my behalf audibly. I needed to hear and see faith in action. Dayshawnna had an intimate relationship with God. She spoke to Him throughout the day, read His word, tithed, and served in several ministries. Obeying and hearing from Him every day were important to her. I, on the other hand, was acquainted with God, meaning I had knowledge of who He is (King of Kings, Redeemer, Healer, Provider, to name a few), but as I mentioned earlier, having knowledge of Him, did not mean that I knew Him. My relationship with God was disturbingly vague and nonspecific. The extent of my interaction involved casually visiting Him periodically on Sundays, stopping by His home, engaging in small talk, chatting with His family members, and rushing out of the sanctuary when the service ended.

During one of my calls with my best friend, she told me I needed to go to God in prayer for myself, which was foreign to me. Outside of the prayers I was taught growing up, I told her I didn't have a clue what to say to God. I didn't know what to pray when my heart was shattered and my mind replayed my trauma.

She went on to tell me that prayer is simply a conversation with God. I told her again, "But I don't know how to pray", and she replied, "It doesn't matter. God likes hearing from you." I wondered why God wanted to hear from me. Me? The one who stopped by casually for a visit, didn't praise or worship Him, and only knew two scriptures in the entire Bible because it was a requirement for Sunday school? Me? The one who spent my life ignoring Him? Me? The one with the unsaved tongue and sinful life? Me? The one who had only prayed once, outside of blessing my food, in twenty-plus years?

I asked her, "Why does he want to hear from me?" She told me God wanted to hear from me because He loves me. It was as if she dropped a lifeline in my lap. After being rejected and feeling unloved by my husband, to hear that God desired to speak with me moved me. To also hear that He loved me regardless of my imperfect state humbled me. It's hard to put in words what I felt at that moment, but I hunched my shoulders forward with relief and smiled on the other end of the phone. My smile was genuine, unlike how I smiled with other people, pretending all was well. It touched and warmed my heart.

Those simple words ignited something in me, which I can only describe as a spiritual stirring. My spirit had been dormant for many years. When I accepted Christ as a teenager, His spirit came to live inside me. And because I didn't take the time to know Him and didn't recognize His voice, His spirit was asleep, waiting. The Bible describes this as spiritual sleepiness, meaning believers who are spiritually dead (Ephesians 5:14).

For more than twenty years, all my decisions were driven by what my flesh wanted, which quieted God's voice. But each time Dayshawnna prayed for me, my spirit stirred. When she told me God wanted to hear from and loved me, my spirit leaped and my faith awakened.

After our call that night, I decided to pray with the hope that I would experience God's peace, comfort, and relief from my emotional distress and mental torment. Needless to say, my prayer wasn't as eloquent or faith filled like as hers, but the important thing was that I tried, and God met me exactly where I was, filled with fear and doubt.

I started with a simple prayer, "God help me." Daily, I replayed the words of my husband wanting to leave and fifteen years of conversations over and over in my head. Not a day went by that I didn't feel the sting of his departure and the feeling that he'd simply moved on with his life unscathed. But when I went to God in prayer, those three words brought a flood of comfort and relief. God didn't want or need me to be like the people I saw in church, nor did He want me to pray like my best friend. He was okay with me being me! He didn't need me to change. I didn't have to stop cursing or lead a sin-free life for God to respond to me—although I eventually scaled down on using profane language to avoid grieving the Holy Spirit. But when I humbly went to God, I did not have to bow, lie prostrate, or kneel in order to reach Him. Instead, I lay down in my bed, curled up in a fetal position with the covers drawn over my head, and I whispered the words, "God help me."

47

The next night, I prayed, "God comfort me." And again, I felt His presence and I got the best night's rest I'd had in months. His comfort, relief, and peace again washed over me. I was so excited about my encounter with God that I shared what I experienced with Dayshawnna. For the first time in my life, He felt real. I didn't have to rely on anyone else's experiences with God. I finally had my own personal experience.

For so long, I'd listened with such reverence to the way other believers spoke of God in their lives. But now I had undeniable evidence of His ability to comfort those in need. His peace washed over my mind and body, and with it came the absence of pain and worry. I discovered I could feel an unexplainable calm while my life was falling apart. It's one thing for someone to tell you how God will comfort you when you feel like you're at the end of your rope, and it's another to have a real-life experience for yourself.

I sounded like a schoolgirl with a crush on a boy. I practically squealed out my excitement when I told Dayshawwna about my encounter with God. She was supportive and said, "God is so awesome. Now it's time for you to read your Bible." She told me that reading God's word would help me know Him on a deeper level and guide me through this difficult ordeal. Admittedly, I wasn't sure how reading about people who lived more than 2,000 years ago would soothe my hurt, but I was open and desperate.

That night, I reached in the drawer of my nightstand and grabbed my Bible. I wasn't sure if I should start in the Old or New Testament. I'd heard some people suggest starting in the Book of Psalm or Proverbs, while others have said to start with the Book of Matthew. Then, a thought that came to mind. I didn't know it at the time, but God was whispering to me that, anytime I read a book, I always started at the beginning, so that's where I started.

I practically devoured every word in the Bible over a period of 3-5 months, from Genesis to Revelation. With each book and chapter, my faith increased and so did my knowledge of God. I read about God and His inexhaustible love for His sons and daughters. I'd listened to my Sunday school teacher tell stories of courageous faith from individuals like Abraham, David, Peter, Paul, and many others, but now I knew for myself how faith should look. Obtaining knowledge about God through His word was easier than I thought and became a priority for the first time in my life, but *knowing* Him required intentional effort on my part.

I read scriptures, took notes, read the commentary and concordance, meditated on what I read, and prayed about what I was reading for more insight. The more that I studied, the more I wanted to know Him outside of the turmoil I was experiencing because of my husband's departure. It didn't matter that I sought God because of my desperate and broken state. It mattered more that my brokenness led me back to Him.

Through my readings, I learned that knowing God meant making the decision in my heart and mind to obey Jesus's teachings and commandments. Simply put, it means saying yes. *Yes, Lord, I will do what you ask even when I don't understand or feel like it, when it does not make sense, or when it goes against how I was raised.* Opening my heart to Him and saying yes was the beginning of my personal relationship with the living God. I moved from being familiar with and having knowledge of Him to deciding to follow and obey Him.

Amazingly, He saw me, not the pretend version of me, but the me I hid from others, and He was filled with love and compassion. He saw beneath the surface and beyond my pretense, and he did not reject me. He didn't see a broken or desperate me but His child whom He loves.

Interestingly, I wanted my husband to see me in the same way as he had when we first met. Picture being on Facebook or Instagram and wanting someone to keep pressing the "like" icon because they saw something you wore, wrote, or posted. Imagine posting something and constantly returning to it to see how many likes you have and who liked or made a comment about your post. Well, that was me. I wanted my husband's love and approval. I wanted him to like what he saw.

Perhaps God withheld my husband's "likes" because I was seeking validation from the wrong person. Maybe God used my husband's departure to redirect me back to Him. What I know is that the more that I wanted God and to spend time in His presence, the less my soul ached.

> *Key Thought:*
> *What if the betrayal and hurt were designed to deepen your knowledge of who God is?*

CHAPTER 4

Season of Anger and Disappointment

*In your anger do not sin. Do not let the sun go down while you are
still angry.*
(Ephesians 4:26)

CONFESSIONS

*L*ord, please restore my marriage. As insane and perhaps
pathetic as my prayer request may sound, given how I was
treated and knowing my husband dated other women during
our marriage, I still went to God in prayer and repeatedly asked Him
to restore my marriage. For weeks, which turned into months, I cried
out daily to God to fix my marriage. I prayed, "Lord, show him. Bring
him back to our family. Create a yearning in his spirit to return home."
I was persistent in my prayers for reconciliation. I was not ashamed of
believing and asking God to heal my relationship.

While I earnestly prayed for God to restore my marriage, two
incidents occurred. First, less than eight months after my husband and
I separated, I discovered he'd filed for divorce. One day, I decided to
search the county public records because the thought crossed my mind
that he might pursue physical custody of our children, and I saw an
open case under my name. The next day, I went to the court to obtain
a copy of what was filed and learned it was a dissolution of marriage.

I was incredibly hurt because he hadn't told me that he planned to file for divorce. I suppose when someone says that they no longer want to be in the marriage, at some point, divorce papers might be filed. However, I honestly thought my husband would have a change of heart and mind after a stint away and would return to our family. After I moved past the feeling of disbelief, I tucked the papers into my folder and walked out of the court house with watery eyes.

The second incident occurred when I went to pick up my children from school. I was approached by the preschool director as I pulled into the driveway. I thought she wanted to discuss an incident with my children or tell me there was an issue with the tuition payment. It was unusual for her to greet me at my car.

As I exited my vehicle, she causally walked toward me and exchanged pleasantries, and then she told me she'd seen my husband with another woman in Aspen. She described the woman as a slim, short African American and mentioned how surprised she was to see him. She also told me that she and my husband spoke to one another, which I suppose was her way of telling me it wasn't a case of mistaken identity.

After she finished, I smiled and told her my husband and I were separated. I can't remember what else we discussed because I felt numb. I saw her lips moving, but my mind went elsewhere. While she provided me with an account of what she'd witnessed, I wondered if she saw the devastation on my face that I felt in my heart. It was as if she'd punched me in the stomach.

After we parted, I went inside to gather my kids and their belongings. I put my children in their car seats, gave them both a juice box, turned on one of their DVDs, and silently cried as I drove home. It was hard for me to believe my husband had moved on so quickly. I thought he was the worst human being alive.

After I arrived home and got my kids settled, I called Dayshawnna to tell her about my conversation with the preschool director. In tears,

I blurted out, "God played me! I thought He would restore my marriage." She said, "Don't say that. God will not push pass someone's will." She proceeded to tell me God couldn't make my husband return to me if that he didn't want to. She described God as a gentleman who allows free will.

I reminded her that, several weeks earlier, God put my marriage on a friend's heart. A friend sent me an email and told me that, while he was praying, the Lord told him to pray for my marriage. This person didn't know my husband and I had separated, but I was so encouraged and thankful that God placed my situation on his heart during prayer. I interpreted this act as God's way of telling me to hold on. I thought restoration of my marriage was near. So when I learned my husband had filed for divorce and was vacationing with another woman in Aspen, I became angry with God.

I asked Dayshwnna, "Why would God do that? Why didn't He save my marriage?" I reminded her that God's will is for the marriage bed to kept pure, undefiled (Hebrews 13:4), but she told me that the scripture was written for believers in Christ and my husband was not a believer. I was so angry that I refused to read my Bible or pray like I did every night. I thought I was hurting God the way that I was hurt.

> *Key Thought:*
> *Wanting something to work and praying about it does not mean it's a part of God's will for your life.*

Have you ever wanted something or someone so badly that, when you didn't get what you wanted, you became angry? Well, I was angry with God! I spent countless hours praying and believing that God would restore my marriage. I walked around my house professing scriptures regarding marriage and how God held marriage in high honor and hated divorce (Malachi 2:16). I studied scriptures relevant to what I was experiencing and read story after story of faith (Hebrews

11:8), reliance (Psalm 46:1-3), dependence (Proverbs 3:5-6), restoration (Job 42:10), redemption (Ephesians 1:7), and victory (1 Corinthians 15:57). I had faith that God was able.

But after both incidents occurred, I perceived that God had failed to act on my behalf, and I lost all hope for my marriage. I arrogantly wondered if God was good, then why didn't this good thing I desperately wanted happen? I could not comprehend my suffering. I incorrectly attributed my husband's failure to return to our marriage to God. The following night, I curled up in my bed and reluctantly reached for my Bible. This time, I did not seek God for comfort or relief, but for answers.

I read from the book of Job, which tells the story of a wealthy man who loses all his children, health, and possessions on the same day. Through his suffering, the Bible implies that he was loathed by his wife and was ridiculed by his friends. Although Job grieved over his losses, his attitude towards God remained positive. One of the most well-known passages in Scripture comes from Job during his season of affliction, which states, "Naked I came from my mother's womb, and naked I will depart. The LORD gave, and the LORD has taken away; may the name of the LORD be praised" (Job 1:21).

But when his grief and suffering continued for several months, he presumptuously began to complain and question God. And while Job did not accuse God of wrongdoing (Job 1:22), he essentially asked Him why did this happen? Instead of answering Job's questions, God presented him with a series of questions (Job 38:1-41) starting with asking, "Where were you when I laid the earth's foundation?" Followed by "Who marked off its dimensions? Surely you know. Who stretched a measuring line across it?" God asked Job more than sixty questions that he was unable to answer.

Before Job's affliction, Satan inaccurately suggested to God that the reason Job was "blameless and upright" in His sight was because God had blessed the work of his hands and therefore his possessions increased (Job 1:8-11). The assumption was that Job was faithful to God because of his blessings and if God removed His protection and allowed Satan to afflict Job by removing all that he loved, that Job would curse God. Satan hoped to reveal that Job loved his blessings from God more than The Source of his blessing, which was not the case. Instead, Job demonstrated his unwavering faith in God.

As I read through the entire book of Job, I heard the Holy Spirit clearly ministering to me. He lovingly told me He was not obligated to answer my questions or give me what I wanted. The underlying question was whether I still loved God even if I didn't get what my heart desired. I had mistakenly correlated God's goodness to positive outcomes in my life and not to His sovereignty, and I felt remorseful. I was humbled by what the Holy Spirit conveyed, and I immediately repented. I said, "Lord forgive me for getting angry with you. Forgive me for my bad attitude. I was wrong and I am sorry." Like Job, I submitted to God's infinite wisdom and at that moment knew He would not withhold anything from me that was good (Psalm 84:11).

At some point in our walk with God, we might question Him or His methods, particularly when things don't go as expected. During those times, we may find ourselves disappointed or angry with Him. Consider when Martha and Mary were disappointed or perhaps upset with Jesus because he didn't arrive soon enough to save their brother Lazarus from dying (John 11:20-21). Think about when David was angry with God when He struck down Uzzah when he reached out to catch the ark of God when the oxen stumbled (2 Samuel 6:6-8). Or Jonah when he became angry with God because he knew that God would extend His mercy to the Ninevites instead of His judgment (Jonah 4:1-3).

God can handle our disappointment and anger. While the Holy Spirit corrected me, God did not abandon or reject me because of the emotions I expressed. I thought, if I earnestly prayed without ceasing about my marriage being restored, the Lord would favorably answer my prayers. Scripture teaches that whatever we pray for, in accordance with His promise, it shall be given (Matthew 18:19). My prayers on the other hand, were not in accordance with God's promise, and He knew what was best for me even though I didn't know it for myself.

In any relationship, you will experience a range of emotions, including disappointment, anger, love, and the list goes on. It's no different with God. I've been told by other believers you should never get angry with God. Well, I disagree. It's natural to be upset with anyone who you have a close and intimate relationship with, including God, but it's more important to tell God how you feel, knowing you can safely take it to Him without fear of rejection and condemnation. When I took my anger and disappointment to God, and He told me He didn't owe me the outcome I sought, I felt His love, mercy, and forgiveness. There, I met God: The God of Mercy and Grace.

> *Key Thought:*
> *The death of something can become a tool that God can use to give birth to something new in your life.*

KNOWING GOD BRINGS REVELATION

The beauty of traveling through different seasons in life is that God will expose ungodly insecurities, perceptions, and attitudes. My experience of being angry with God revealed five things about me.

1. Entitlement

First, God exposed my attitude of entitlement. I thought praying earnestly, attempting to live in accordance to God's word, attending church regularly, and tithing entitled me to what I sought. My faith was formulaic. If I did this, then God would do that. But God gives out of His abundance because of who He is and not because of what I do. Further, I believed that I was entitled to relief. I spent months feeling

56

afraid, abandoned, and rejected, and I expected God to remove my suffering. The pain of being separated from my husband was agonizing and I expected God to do something about it. God heard all my prayers and pleas for reconciliation, but He never promised to restore my marriage. While I thanked and was grateful to Him for blessing me with health, healthy children, and a place to live that I could afford, I focused on what I wanted and what I did not have.

2. Distorted View on Marriage and Love

Second, God showed me I had a distorted view on marriage and love. My petition to God to restore my marriage was about what I wanted and not what God wanted for me. *I* wanted my husband back, *I* wanted our children to live in a house with both parents, *I* wanted a husband who treated his family as a priority, *I* wanted companionship, and *I* did not want to feel lonely any longer. However, God showed me being married wasn't about me, how I felt, or filling some void that I had in my life. Marriage is designed for Him. Marriage should bring glory to God. It represents God's love, and the fruit of the marital union is godly children (Malachi 2:15).

When God and His love are at the center of marriage, even when couples have difficulty, He can sustain you and bring peace and grace to you and your spouse because He loves you. When God is not at the center of marriage, it can result in unexplainable emptiness or even divorce. In my case, God was not at the center of my marriage.

God further revealed that my view on love conflicted with Christ's love. In my heart, I loved my husband with great intensity. But did I mistake the intensity of what I felt for him as an indication of love? When I lined up my version of love with the word of God, it was clear I had strong feelings for my husband, but it did not reflect love as described in 1 Corinthians 13.

The Bible describes love as unselfishly kind and an unconditional act that is not reciprocated. "For God so loved the world that he gave his one and only Son." (John 3:16). He gave unselfishly, fully knowing we couldn't reciprocate what He gave. But my love was conditional. It was predicated on how I felt and what I thought. My love was compromising, impatient, and at times, sharp. I'm not trying to convince you or myself that I didn't love my husband, which I certainly did. I'm simply describing some of the thoughts God later revealed. In essence, my version of love was defined by culture (conditional and self-satisfying) and in opposition to His word.

Pastor Dharius Daniel preached in one of his sermons that Jesus was the walking example of what real love should look like in the life of believers, how love behaves whether it's reciprocated or not, and how we should respond despite how others choose to act. When the Holy Spirit downloaded some of these things to me through scripture and various sermons, I saw that I had a distorted and dysfunctional concept of what it meant to love someone. Over the years, God had to teach me how to love, not the way I spoke of loving my husband, but reflecting the love of Christ (patient, kind, long-suffering, never fails, does not envy or boast, does not keep a record of wrong-doing).

3. Mourning What God Rejected

Third, God revealed I was mourning someone He had rejected for me. Consider the story of how Samuel mourned for Saul when God tore Saul's kingdom away from him (1 Samuel 13:7-14) because of his disobedience (1 Samuel 15:10-35). In 1 Samuel 16:1, "The Lord said to Samuel, 'How long will you mourn for Saul, since I have rejected him as king over Israel? Fill your horn with oil and be on your way; I am sending you to Jesse of Bethlehem. I have chosen one of his sons to be king.'"

While God honors the covenant of marriage (Matthew 19:6) and calls for the marriage bed to be undefiled (Hebrews 13:4), the scripture says regarding the principle of marriage, "But if the unbeliever leaves, let it be so. The brother or the sister is not bound in such circumstances; God has called us to live in peace" (1 Corinthians 7:15). In my case, my husband was an unbeliever. I don't believe God orchestrated my broken marriage, but after my husband decided to leave, He wanted me to move forward with my life and release my husband and marriage in my heart.

I spent so much time mourning over what was lost that I didn't see I should have been fighting instead for my children, so they would never have to see their mother tolerate lies, compromise values, accept infidelity, or endure what I did because of a twisted and ungodly idea of love. At some point, we must all ask ourselves what we are mourning over that God has rejected. Perhaps God was saying to me, "How long will you mourn over him? I have rejected him. I need you to move forward. Where I am taking you, you do not need him."

4. Warped Discernment and Pride

God revealed that my desire to stay in my marriage was so strong that it interfered with my ability to discern that it ended years before my husband decided to leave. Discernment is from the Holy Spirit and it allows me to see and detect. He leads, alerts, warns, and directs me to biblical truths. When I accepted Jesus, the Holy Spirit came to reside in me. However, in my youth and during a clunk of my adult life, before I decided to follow Christ, I did not recognize His voice, which meant that I could not discern His will. Looking back, the Holy Spirit alerted me that my marriage was in trouble and my husband had deceptive behaviors and intentions, but I shrugged Him off. There were things I didn't detect in my marriage, which is why I felt blindsided and ambushed by my husband's announcement. The lines were blurred between how I was raised and what I desired most.

God also showed me pride kept me in a place and state of mind I needed to move past. Loyalty and commitment were concepts I embraced and valued so much that I convinced myself walking away was unthinkable. I'd poured so much into my marriage that I refused to abandon it or admit that the relationship was over despite the clear signs.

5. Idolatry and Worship

The fifth thing the Lord revealed was that I idolized and worshiped my husband. An idol is a person, object, or thing that has a higher priority in your heart than God. Whatever we meditate on day and night is an idol. It's dangerous to dismiss the idea that we can't idolize or worship people. It happened to me subtly. It started with what I saw (a potential spouse), then moved on to what I thought I had to have (marriage), and finally ended with what I thought I could not live without (my husband).

Speaking with a friend, I compared my attraction and love for my husband to a snake charmer and his snake. My husband's words were the flute he used to mesmerize and lure me. It felt as if I was under a spell when he was near. I shared with her that I was intoxicated by his presence and his gaze was hypnotic. There were times when my body swayed when he was speaking as if I heard music in my head. I also shared that his voice and the words he spoke were alluring and the texture of his voice was warm and soothing, like silk, soft to my skin. I sought him for wisdom, comfort, provision, and encouragement. I looked to him to satisfy whatever need I had. So when he left, it felt like he took a part of me with him. I thought my life would crumble without him in it.

At the time, I didn't see anything wrong with how I described my attraction for my husband or how I behaved, however the Lord revealed to me that my thoughts, behaviors, and description constituted a form of idol worship. Consider how God instructed the Israelites to have no other gods before Him, to not make an image in the form of anything, and not to bow down to images or worship them (Exodus 20:3-5). Despite the many wonders they witnessed when God delivered them from bondage, over time, idols took the place of God in their hearts. Ask yourself: "What has taken God's place in my heart?" Perhaps it's your family, job, car, money, possessions, status, acknowledgment, social media, exercise, TV, recognition, or music, to name a few.

In my heart, I bowed to my husband before and during our marriage, not literally, but spiritually. I worshiped the words he spoke and his intelligence, wit, and talents. I put my husband on the throne of my heart, which God needed to correct. He didn't design the institution of marriage for believers to idolize and worship our spouse. While there was nothing wrong with being attracted to my spouse and admiring his attributes, there's a problem when we put our spouse and marriage ahead of our relationship with God. If God reveals through prayer that you have erected idols in your heart, ask Him to help you dethrone them.

Life Lesson #5
Don't idealize what or who God has delivered you from.

KNOWING GOD EXPOSES WRONG CHOICES

I had unknowingly lived a life of deception. Deception occurs when we believe we are operating in truth but the reality is that we're not. The problem with being deceived is that it's not always easily detectable, which is why believers are warned to be on guard (1 Peter

5:8). The enemy, the devil, is described in the Bible like a roaring lion, prowling around looking for someone to swallow (1 Peter 5:8). In other words, the devil is actively looking to deceive and exploit our weaknesses. While there are many instances of deception in the Bible, the most poignant example is the story of Adam and Eve when Satan deceived Eve into eating the fruit from the tree of the knowledge of good and evil, which God forbade (Genesis 2:16-17). If Eve, a woman who walked with God, could be easily deceived, then we, whether we believe in God or not, are susceptible to deception.

Unequally Yoked

When my husband and I began dating, the first question my mother asked me was whether he was a Christian or not. I thought she was being dramatic and old-fashioned. "What's the big deal if I want to date someone who doesn't believe in God?" I thought. I told her, "As long as he's not a devil worshiper, I'm okay with it." I told her it was enough that I believed in God, but she warned me not to date an unbeliever. She told me we were unequally yoked (2 Corinthians 6:13-15). I later realized she meant I shouldn't yoke myself—become emotionally, physically, or spiritually attached—with an unbeliever because he could turn me away from Christ. She also knew my walk with God would be corrupted by an unbeliever (1 Corinthians 15:33). At the time, I didn't know God or the value of being obedient to His word.

In scripture, God warns the children of Israel not to marry women from other nations because they would turn their hearts towards the gods of those nations and away from Him (1 Kings 11:2). God gave this command for their own protection. Yet, they intermarried and worshiped other gods (1 Kings 11:3). The Bible also points out that King Solomon held on to his love for his seven hundred foreign wives and three hundred concubines, who led him astray, and his devotion to

God dwindled (1 Kings 11:3-6). And like the children of Israel and King Solomon, I yoked myself with an unbeliever and my heart turned away from God. I dated someone who didn't attend church or pray to God, which made my decision to not attend or not pray easier. My husband also believed a person's religious beliefs shouldn't be forced upon others, which at the time made sense, so I considered not exposing my children to God or "forcing" them to attend church because of how I was raised.

Dating an unbeliever moved my thoughts and heart further and further from God. I deceived myself into believing that dating an unbeliever didn't matter if we loved each other. I thought it was more important to date someone who was supportive, kind, smart and understanding, made me laugh, and was a good provider. If there was harmony, I thought, then it didn't matter if we shared the same faith or not. I was wrong. I didn't understand the ramifications of my choice.

My heart and mind were so entangled with my soon-to-be husband that I didn't listen to the wisdom my mother offered. And when I failed to heed her advice, God sent someone else to bring me wisdom and a word of warning about dating a non-believer. One of my co-workers, Trinity was a believer. Daily, she chased after me about getting to know God and not yoking myself with an unbeliever. She hounded me so relentlessly I wondered if my mother had sent her.

One day, Trinity shared that she married an unbeliever, and she described the many challenges she experienced that ultimately led to their divorce. After her divorce, she encountered God, and He transformed her life and lifestyle through His word. She went on to share that, after God delivered her from hurt, she later married a believer. And while they had challenges like most couples, it was different because they both put God at the center of their marriage.

Trinity didn't want me to make the same mistake and encouraged me to seek God through His word. I told her I didn't understand God's word because it was filled with too much "thou shalt" and "ye". A few

63

days later, she handed me the Life Application Bible. It was easy to read and understand. No more excuses!

As I started reading God's word, I felt convicted about my dating choice, but I wasn't ready to walk away. As I read more, I felt more uneasy. I started to have doubts about remaining in my relationship. While I was struggling to decide if I would stay or leave, my soon-to-be-husband proposed. Keep in mind that marrying him was my greatest desire at the time, so I said yes. I wrongly reasoned in my mind that God wanted me to be happy and my soon-to-be husband made me happy. Yet, I never found any scriptures in the Bible that spoke about God wanting believers to be happy. He wants us to experience His joy and peace and to live a blessed life.

Although my answer to the proposal was yes, I still wanted to know if I should marry him. So I asked God, and in my heart, He told me no. He didn't yell the words, but he gave me an unmistakable no! Outside of saying grace, this was the one time I prayed in twenty years. And when I sought God's will, and He told me no, I slammed the Bible shut and didn't pick it up again until my husband left me.

One of my favorite YouTube preachers, Pastor Dharius Daniels, said if God cannot teach you through His instruction, He will let you learn your lesson through experience. Well, I learned many lessons because I ignored the warnings from the Lord. Two different people warned me not to date the person I chose, but I didn't listen. And when I sought God regrading whether I should marry my husband or not, I disregarded His counsel, and had to live with the choice I made.

Marriage Choice

I've heard many pastors say, and I agree, that God does not choose who we marry. Throughout Scripture, human beings chose who they married. God brought Eve to Adam (Genesis 2:23), but He allowed Adam to choose her. Samson chose his first Philistine wife (Judges

64

14:1-2) and later chose Delilah (Judges 16:4), which ultimately led to his destruction. King Solomon, the wisest man to ever live (1 Kings 4:29-30), actively sought out unbelieving wives, which led him to worship other gods (1 Kings 11).

God is a God of order and intention, which is seen throughout Genesis 1 and 2 when He creates a world of beauty and abundance for man to enjoy. He cares about everything regarding us (Psalm 37:23), including who we choose to marry, and so He calls believers to be equally yoked (2 Corinthians 6:14). I chose to be with someone who wasn't a part of God's promise. I wanted someone who God knew would one day leave me, and I asked Him to keep me yoked to that person even though he defiled our marriage vows. Matthew 7:9-10 says, "Which of you, if your son asks for bread, will give him a stone? Or if he asks for a fish, will give him a snake?" Consider that God, as our Father, loves you and me too much to grant us something that will ultimately harm us and our purpose.

Life Lesson #6
God will not present someone to you for marriage who contradicts His word.

Marrying my husband was something I desired from the moment I met him. I set my sights and heart on becoming his wife. The person I choose didn't possess godly character, nor was he a believer in Christ. Instead of choosing someone I thought was witty, articulate, and charming, in hindsight, I should have followed the advice from wise counsel and aligned my choice with God's word. Instead, I experienced unnecessary heartache, and my self-worth plummeted.

While God did not decide who I married, He was with me through all the grief, rejection, and sorrow. Knowing Him more intimately taught me to discern His voice, understand the importance of obedience, seek godly counsel when I'm uncertain, and align whatever choices I make with His word. I'm not suggesting that marrying a believer means life will be free of trouble because trouble will come (John 16:33). There are plenty of marriages between believers that end in divorce for many reasons. However, I believe the word of God should be our compass and advice from godly counsel when deciding who to marry.

Years later, my anger and disappointment brought about revelations that I didn't initially see. I desperately wanted God to restore my marriage and for reconciliation to occur, but He wanted to reconcile me back to Him. I had gone astray and was lost. I unknowingly thought my husband's absence would destroy me, but God used my wrong choices, like the prodigal son, to bring me back to Christ, and I will forever be thankful.

CHAPTER 5
Season of Restored Sight

For our struggle is not against flesh and blood, but against the rulers, against the authorities, against the powers of this dark world and against the spiritual forces of evil in the heavenly realms.
(Ephesians 6:12)

BLINDED BY REJECTION

Experiencing the end of a marriage is life altering. You cannot go through life with someone who you've given your entire self to without being scarred psychologically and emotionally when they choose to end the relationship. Discovering they've given a part of themselves to someone else is equally damaging.

It was hard for me to absorb how my life changed so dramatically in a matter of moments. I reluctantly accepted the death of a dream and moved into my new reality of single motherhood and living apart from my husband, realizing that reconciliation of my marriage was not in my future. Some days, I couldn't pull myself out of the bed. I felt like I was drowning in grief. There were times when I was overcome with sadness and told my children we were taking a day off school and work, which they happily celebrated. Meanwhile, I pulled the covers over my head and cried so much I thought my heart would burst.

My soul was troubled when I was awake, remembering when he sat next to me, his hands folded, his head lowered, and the dreaded announcement that he no longer wanted to remain in the marriage. His words were like a broken record and my mind kept pressing the replay button. I could not understand how someone who declared to love me in front of our family, friends, and God "for better or worse, sicker or poorer, until death do us part," could treat me like a used car he decided to trade in because newer models with sleek designs, new technologies, and fewer miles were available. Perhaps my exterior had a few dings and imperfections, and my overall value had depreciated in his eyes.

The pain of his absence was so severe that it gripped my heart. All I saw and felt was devastation, suffering, and disbelief. My abilities to process, express how I felt, and cope were challenged. The only time I felt relief outside of prayer was when I was asleep. I knew I wasn't perfect, but I was faithful and loyal, which I thought would count for something. I loved my husband, but it was clear that whatever love he possessed for me had been extinguished. His demeanor towards me was cold and distant. Contempt replaced the love and compassion he once held in his eyes. There were no visible signs that the end of our marriage hurt him, nor did he express remorse or regret.

When he left, it broke my confidence, resolve, and resiliency. I felt exposed and vulnerable. I dealt with difficult emotions, including sorrow, depression, and denial. Every emotion was amplified and turned inward, including my anger. Normally, when I'm upset, my contorted expression, stiff posture, and fierce words are aimed at someone specific. Instead, I held my anger inside, where it percolated. I was afraid, if I let it out, I would be consumed by bitterness.

There were days when my mind raced over my perceived failures as a wife and my feelings engulfed me. At times, it felt like I was free-falling, and other times, like I was drowning. I had difficulty persuading my mind to slow down, so I could digest and process the magnitude of what I felt, which made me overwhelmingly exhausted. I struggled daily to fight against negative thoughts I had about myself.

The words I spoke aloud were self-deprecating. I told myself I wasn't good enough, pretty enough, nurturing enough, or career-focused enough. I did not see my own self-worth.

God knew I didn't have an accurate picture of myself. He also knew the betrayal, rejection, and abandonment had stolen my spiritual sight, my ability to accurately see the enormity of who God is. My eyes were covered in shame and regret, which blinded me from seeing spiritual truths about myself. But before God dealt with my vision, He needed to teach me how to silence my thoughts and fortify my mind.

DEBILITATING THOUGHTS AND LIMITING BELIEFS

This was the most depressing season of my life. I saw myself as worthless; a person whose husband left because I had deficiencies. I told myself it was my fault that he left, that I should have tried harder. I no longer saw myself as strong, self-assured, and brave but rather as wimpy, trepid, and wary. I developed the habit of downplaying or dismissing compliments because I didn't believe I deserved them.

On a trip to the mall with my best friend, we went inside a lingerie store, mainly to browse and try on intimate apparel. I stood in the mirror and told her how unattractive I felt. I criticized my body and overall appearance. I told her I was disgusted by what I saw in the mirror. Naturally, she reassured me of my beauty and worth, but I couldn't see whatever she saw at the time. All I saw was a flawed me.

Each morning, I'd get into my car and try to avoid looking at myself in the mirror because I felt disgusted with myself. Every blemish, line, and imperfection were magnified. In my heart, I told myself I was ugly. I wondered if my husband left because I lacked something. Perhaps I wasn't quiet or docile enough. Maybe he liked my spark and electric style when we dated but grew weary of me over time. There was no need for anyone else to reject me because I did a good job of rejecting and ridiculing myself.

God heard the words I spoke out loud and in my heart. In my spirit, I heard the Lord tell me to stop speaking negative words about myself. He knows the power of words, if used in the wrong way, bring destruction (Proverbs 15:4, 18:7, 18:21). But first, God wanted to adjust and align my thinking to scripture. He wanted to give me a revelation of my *who*.

WHO AM I?

I had forgotten who I was. I was lost in depressing thoughts. My who was interwoven with my husband and without him, I no longer knew myself. Fortunately, the Bible is filled with people who did not recognize their who and spoke negative words about themselves. And each time, God reminded them of wh*o* He created them to be. Think about how Jeremiah told the Lord that he did not know how to speak on His behalf because he was too young after God told him who he was. Jeremiah was the Lord's chosen messenger to bring His word to the children of Israel. He was anointed by God for that very reason. After God told Jeremiah who he was, He dealt with how he described himself. "But the Lord said to me, 'Do not say, 'I am too young.' You must go to everyone I send you to and say whatever I command you" (Jeremiah 1:7). While it was true that Jeremiah was young, the Lord wanted to correct how he saw himself. Jeremiah did not see his worth.

Similarly, the angel of the Lord challenged Gideon's view of himself and reinforced his who by calling him a mighty hero when Gideon saw himself as weak, afraid, and the least in his father's house (Judges 6:15). Before God released Jeremiah or Gideon to carry out His will, He first addressed their who and then what they thought and said about themselves. Along those same lines, the Lord had to deal with me in both areas.

To address the loss of my who and restore my sight to what the Lord originally gave me, I looked at scripture. According to His word,

70

He knit me together in my mother's womb (Psalm 139:13) and created me in His own image (Genesis 1:27). God called me His masterpiece (Ephesians 2:10) and the apple of His eye (Zechariah 2:8). He showed me I was fearfully and wonderfully made (Psalm 139:14) and that I am strong (Psalm 18:32). He reminded me I am His child (John 1:12) and He has taken care of me since birth and will continue to do so when I am old (Isaiah 46:3-4). He told me He is always near when I'm crushed and brokenhearted (Psalm 34:18), that I'm never out of His sight (Psalm 139:3), and nothing or no one can separate me from His love (Romans 8:38-39). Most importantly, He revealed He loves me so much that He sent Jesus to die for my sins (John 3:16).

In essence, He loves me no matter what. He's made up His mind about me. He will not waiver in His love for me. He will not reject me as long as I love and pursue Him. He understands me and has not required perfection from me.

It took me several months of absorbing, meditating, and embracing the way in which I was described in scripture to move from self-doubt to self-love. In hindsight, I believe God wanted my who to be intertwined with Him and what He said about me. And during that time, He taught me to follow Him, His ways, and His voice. And after He reminded me of my who, then He dealt with my thoughts and words.

WINNING THE BATTLE OVER THOUGHTS AND WORDS

Your beliefs become your thoughts,
your thoughts become your words,
your words become your habits,
your habits become your values,
your values become your destiny. – Unknown

Words we speak about ourselves are a powerful weapon that can be used for or against us. My beliefs that I was unworthy, less than, and a failure were curses I professed over myself. I cannot tell you how many times I rehearsed and uttered disparaging words about myself. But to be healed from tormenting beliefs, I had to change which voice that I chose to listen to in my head.

> ### Life Lesson # 7
> *Watch what you believe and say about yourself.*

Steps to Control Your Thoughts and Words

Meditating on God's word was one way that helped to silence the negative words I said and how I saw myself. The other ways included professing His word, reminding God of the promises he made to His people, and giving myself permission to experience His peace.

Step 1: Meditate on His word.

In the book of Psalms (1:1-3), David declares that those who delight in the law of the Lord and meditate on the law, day and night, are like trees planted by streams of water and bearing fruit. Their leaves never wither and whatever they do will prosper. David points out that in the presence of God there is growth, maturity, nourishment, and prosperity as we drink from His word, and we bear fruit—love, joy, peace, forbearance, kindness, goodness, faithfulness, gentleness, and self-control (Galatians 5:22-23). Like the roots of a tree that grow deep into the soil when they're watered, so do our faith and understanding of God's "who" and of His will grow deep in His presence.

Think about when God told Joshua to meditate on His word day and night and keep his commandments so that Joshua would prosper (Joshua 1:8). In the books of Psalms and Joshua, God promises

72

prosperity *if* we meditate on His word and do not depart from it. While some may interpret prosperity to mean financial gain, what it meant to me was transformed thoughts and emotional relief. As I meditated on God's word and found strength in His presence, I told myself I was enough. Instead of avoiding the mirror in my car, in His presence I recited aloud that I was beautiful, remarkable, extraordinary, strong, and loved. More importantly, I reminded myself that I was not a failure. Perhaps this is why Paul urged believers to take every thought captive unto the obedience of Christ (2 Corinthians 10:5), meaning to bring every thought under submission, and to think on things which are true, noble, lovely, and pure (Philippians 4:8). I had to remind myself that Satan is the father of lies (John 8:44) and his job is to steal, kill, and destroy (John 10:10). He wanted to destroy how I saw myself. He wanted me to believe I was insignificant and to meditate day and night on my perceived failures instead of meditating on God's word.

Two voices vied to win my thoughts. One voice, God's voice, called me bold, beautiful, and the apple of His eye, while the other called me weak, unworthy, and a failure. Whichever voice is the strongest and the one you meditate on the most is the one that rules your thoughts.

Step 2: Profess God's word over your situation and remind Him of His promises.

Speaking the Word out loud helped me take control of my mouth. I walked around my house professing scriptures over myself and my life in accordance with His word. Paraphrasing, I said, "I am the head and not the tail, above and not beneath" (Deuteronomy 28:13); "I will lend to many nations, but will not borrow" (Deuteronomy 15:6); "God will give me beauty instead of ashes" (Isaiah 61:3); "You will give me a double recompense for my former shame" (Isiah 61:7); and "I am more than a conqueror in Christ Jesus" (Romans 8:37).

But why did I profess God's word aloud? Scripture teaches believers to bring God in remembrance of His word (Isaiah 43:26) to remind Him of the many promises He made His people. When God gives instructions to remind Him of His word, we should do it because His word is alive, active, and sharper than a two-edged sword (Hebrews 4:12). Both Nehemiah (Nehemiah 1:8-11) and King Jehoshaphat (2 Chronicles 20:6-7) reminded God of His promises aloud, and He answered.

I also brought another prayer to God which helped discipline my thought life. I prayed, "Lord, you said you would restore the years the locusts had eaten" (Joel 2:25). This scripture speaks to when Israel's crops were destroyed by locusts, which took several years for an abundant harvest to be produced. But God promised that He would restore what they lost. When I read this scripture, I thought of the fifteen years of dating and being married to my husband that I'd lost and would never get back. I reminded God of His promise, prayed that He'd restore my lost years, and believed He would bring abundance into my life, which He has done day after day and year after year.

Reciting and believing in the power of God's word is critical to casting out debilitating thoughts and changing what you say. Equally important are speaking His truth, and not the lies of the enemy, and applying scripture to your situation.

When I walked around my house speaking God's word, transformation happened in my mind and heart. I didn't realize at the time that He was changing and cleaning my heart and mind from the inside out. Surprisingly, I'd never known I could take control over my thoughts and words. However, the more time I spent in His presence, the more I grew spiritually and His truth about me became my truth.

Step 3: Experience His peace.

I had to condition myself to keep my mind focused on God (Colossians 3:2), which brought peace (Isaiah 26:3). When I fixated on my failed marriage, the words from my husband, and the pain, I didn't have peace. Instead, I felt anxious, regretful, shameful, and worried. But when I kept my mind set on God and listened, I had peace and my thoughts were under the control of the Holy Spirit.

I had a choice to make; either I was going to believe how I felt, what I thought, and what other people said or I would believe the One who cannot lie (Numbers 23:19). I chose the latter. It was not easy to quiet my mind and use God's word, especially because I'd fallen into the habit of using self-deprecating words as a result of rejection. It was a daily fight to choose what God said about me, but each day, with God's help, the incapacitating thoughts subsided. Once I absorbed all God was revealing to help quiet my thoughts, which took a year or more, my mind was strengthened and fortified.

CHAPTER 6
Season of Trust and Obedience

Trust in the LORD with all your heart and lean not on your own understanding; in all your ways submit to him, and he will make your paths straight. Do not be wise in your own eyes; fear the LORD, and shun evil.
(Proverbs 3)

BETRAYAL

Knowing I'd misjudged my husband made me afraid of letting anyone else near my heart. I didn't want to experience that type of betrayal again. I was suspicious of all men and terrified they were dishonest cheaters. I believed their motives were impure and they sought to add me to their list of relationship casualties. I no longer felt I had the luxury to be cavalier with my emotions and interactions. As such, I became overly cautious and guarded, so I placed a fortified, impenetrable wall around my heart to protect and shield me from hurt.

Paul warned believers to guard their hearts—the mind, will, and emotions—because from the heart springs forth the issues of life (Proverbs 4:23). I misinterpreted this scripture to mean I needed to encase my heart to prevent further suffering. But another interpretation is to keep watch or be on guard so my heart isn't filled with ungodly thoughts and words because everything I do will give birth to spiritual blessings or curses. God revealed that there's a difference between building a wall around my heart to prevent someone from entering and erecting a fence. A wall by design is tall to keep others out and protect those people or things within, whereas fences are made for privacy. Walls around the heart block the blessings of God and His truth, but fences allow access by invitation.

The thought of someone betraying me, breaking my heart again, and damaging my self-esteem was frightening. I didn't want to ever feel defenseless, lose my identity, or be taken advantage of again by anyone. A part of me wanted to hide, settle for being alone, and pour myself into my children and work to avoid trusting someone new in my life.

I wondered when I'd become a scaredy-cat. I'm sure if you were to ask someone from my past to use a word to describe me, scary wouldn't be high on the list. But there I was, fearful of being betrayed and deceived. Admittedly, I'd been betrayed and deceived by close friends, family, and acquaintances before, but it wasn't until my husband left, that I experienced the type of betrayal and deception that crippled and practically incapacitated me. When you experience this form of duplicity, trust does not come easy.

God reminded me in His word that betrayal will come even from those who I trust (Psalm 41: 9). But take heart, Jesus, Joseph, and many others endured and survived betrayal and so would I. He told me I didn't need to be afraid of being betrayed again because He heals broken hearts. And although my heart was shattered when my marriage ended, God put every piece of it back together. In doing so, He showed me I could survive heartache again because He is my shield and my refuge, and in Him I can always find protection. Psalm 56: 3-4 says,

When I am afraid,
I put my trust in you.

In God, whose word I praise—
in God I trust and am not afraid.
What can mere mortals do to me?

To move beyond hurt, suspicion, and betrayal required trusting God. So in faith, I gave God access to my heart and opened myself up to the possibility of being duped again. Trusting Him required complete surrender. Initially, I was reluctant, but I also knew I didn't want to sit on the sidelines of life. I wanted to find love again or at least have it find me. But relationships are built on trust, and I struggled in this area.

Trusting Him in Dating Relationships

When I told God I was afraid to trust again because of past hurts, I heard the Holy Spirit say, "I'm not asking you to trust a man. I am asking you to *trust me* concerning man." There was no doubt in my mind that I trusted God, but I wasn't exactly sure what He meant about trusting Him concerning men until He quickened my spirit. First, He told me to trust all men who I chose to date.

What did you say Jesus? Did you say trust all *men who I choose to date?* I had a problem with this. Growing up, I was taught that trust was earned and should not be easily given. I thought people should prove they were trustworthy by keeping their word, demonstrating integrity, and committing to honesty. The idea of trusting someone first sounded insane. While this may be a practice for some women and men, it wasn't my practice.

Second, He told me to give men who I chose to date the benefit of the doubt. He wanted me to not assume every man was a liar. I wondered if I'd heard God correctly. *Why would I make the ridiculous assumption that men who I choose to date are honest?* Perhaps I could give someone the benefit of the doubt after knowing him for a while,

79

but not when we first started dating. No thanks! I wasn't comfortable or presumptuous enough to believe all men were honest. I wanted to shout God down and say, "Nope, I'm not doing it! I will not let anyone else deceive me again."

While I trusted God, I still struggled with Him telling me to trust men I chose to date and give them the benefit of the doubt. In my heart, I screamed, "I did that already!" Perhaps He knew that if I didn't let go of hurt and mistrust, I'd carry those fears and feelings and project them into my future interactions with men. God wanted me to be whole again in every area of my life. He didn't want me to live in bondage and fear of being hurt. But the question I needed to answer for myself was whether I trusted God in all areas or only some areas of my life.

Life Lesson #8
Trusting God in relationships does not mean throwing wisdom out the window. It means listening to the Holy Spirit every step of the way whether you understand God's direction or not.

Why did God ask me to trust Him concerning men? I believe He wanted me to trust Him, knowing He was with me and would protect me. He wanted me to cast my concerns, worries, and fears upon Him. It's important to remember, as I've mentioned, that hurt, and betrayal will come your way. It's unavoidable. However, Psalm 91 describes the hedge of protection over my life and assures me that the Lord loves and will rescue me from harm. What this looks like practically is that when I'm hurt in relationships, I know that God always "has my back" and will deliver me from a state of broken heartedness.

Trusting God concerning men also means:

1. Submitting my whole heart with full obedience and reverence, despite what I think or feel.
2. Acknowledging His wisdom and believing He knows what's best for my life.

80

3. Seeking His guidance and waiting for Him to prompt my spirit rather than taking matters into my own hands.

4. Following His instructions.

5. Believing His plans for my life are good.

Although I wrestled with God's instruction to trust first because it went against all I knew, transformation and mind renewal wouldn't have happened if I'd chosen my way instead of His. As I relied more on God in my dating relationships and followed the instructions He provided, I was no longer afraid of being hurt. Further, I stopped feeling suspicious of men I dated and learned to quickly give them the benefit of the doubt. Whatever concerns I had about trust in relationships dissipated.

> *Key Thought:*
> *If you do not trust God in your dating relationships, you will trust in yourself and your own thoughts.*

Trusting Him Concerning My Children

God told me to let go of my children—to release them. *Yep, nope!* That was not going to happen. One day, my husband called and wanted the children to spend the weekend at his new apartment, so he could introduce them to his new girlfriend. This was the same woman from his office who he'd denied having an affair with while we were married. I later discovered she also left her marriage. And my husband wanted to parade around his new relationship without considering whether the timing to introduce someone new to our children was appropriate or not. If I'm being completely honest, at that moment, I wanted the Lord to send fire from heaven to swallow him up.

I was appalled. He wanted our children, who did not understand why their daddy no longer lived with us or why we moved out of our home, to meet his mistress. I didn't know this woman or how she would treat my children. I didn't trust him or her. Aside from those feelings, I questioned whether my husband would be attentive and watchful there had been times when he was absent-minded.

I hung on to my children for dear life after my husband left. Instinctually, I felt my role was to serve as their protector, provider, and nurturer, but that role belonged for God. When the Lord told me to release them to my husband, I cried like a baby. I prayed and told the Lord, "Father, he does not deserve to have access to our kids. Look how he treated us. He left us. He doesn't even ask how they're doing. He doesn't deserve to be in their presence. I don't trust him with the kids, Lord." Again, God told me He wasn't asking me to trust my husband; He was asking me to trust Him with the well-being of my children.

OBEDIENCE IS BETTER THAN SACRIFICE

But why did I need to release them to my husband to show I trusted God? Trusting God requires obedience. Perhaps He was testing me, like He did Abraham (Genesis 22:1-19), to see if I would withhold my children from Him. Because Abraham trusted God and did not withhold his son, God promised to bless his descendants and make them as numerous as the stars, and every nation on earth would be blessed through his offspring (Genesis 22:16-18).

In the book of Philippians 4:18, a sacrifice is described as a fragrant offering, pleasing to God. Jesus offered himself up as a fragrant offering to God and sacrificed himself because He loves us (Ephesians 5:2). Keep in mind, my desire was to know God more intimately. But that requires sacrifice. God gave His son as a sacrifice for our sins to show us the depth of His love. While I didn't have to watch anyone mistreat, abuse, or crucify my children the way God did with Jesus, in my heart, I connected with God in a new way. What better way to know God than to trust Him by sacrificing my most precious gift and offering that gift back to Him? Intimacy requires trust and sacrifice. The more we trust, the closer we become. Ask yourself what or who are you willing to sacrifice in your heart and give back to God?

I knew and know God's love and protection reach beyond my imagination and it was He who gifted me with my beautiful children. When I released my children into God's hands, and obeyed the Holy Spirit, offering them as a fragrant offering, an enormous burden was lifted from me. My act of obedience took my prayer life to a higher level and my trust in God abounded. Instead of praying and asking God to change my husband's heart toward me and the kids and to allow him to see the hurt and trauma caused by his selfish desires, I prayed that God create in me a clean heart (Psalm 51:10). I knew I didn't have the power to change my husband, and he was content with the choices he'd made, so I asked God to change me. I asked Him to search my heart and remove anything unlike Christ.

I expected to spend the weekend anxious and stressed, wondering if my husband was taking care of our children and if they'd cry because I wasn't around. But it was one of the most relaxing weekends I ever had. I didn't worry about my children and my mind didn't wander off to some dark place. I had peace in my heart and mind after following His instructions. I reminded myself that His ways are not my ways and His thoughts are not my thoughts (Isaiah 55:8).

GOD'S INSTRUCTION

My trust-walk and my act of obedience with God taught me that He is a God of instruction, which is found in His word. Think about how God gave detailed instructions to the children of Israel for every aspect of life. When they obeyed His instructions, they experienced victory and rest from their enemies. But when they wandered off, ignored God, and pursued their desires, they experienced death, defeat, and curses (Deuteronomy 28).

I discovered trusting Him means obeying His instructions quickly and fully, not partially. Noah demonstrated full obedience when God gave him specific instructions for building the ark, and he obeyed (Genesis 6). However, Saul partially obeyed the Lord's instruction (1 Samuel 15:1-9). Partial obedience is hearing whatever you want to hear and doing whatever you want to do instead of submitting to what God has instructed. In Saul's case, the Lord condemned his partial obedience as an act of disobedience and rejected him as king (1 Samuel 15:23).

Partial obedience would have been me telling my husband, "Yes, you can pick up the kids in a month, and no, you cannot introduce them to your new girlfriend." Well, God clearly told me to release my children, which meant immediately. He never said to interfere with my husband's interest in introducing my kids to this woman (partial obedience). So many times, I wanted to interfere and ignore what God instructed me to do because I believed I was protecting my children from emotional and psychological harm. But if I planned to follow God completely, it meant not treating His word and commandments like they were optional.

Paul warned believers about strongholds, mindsets and reasoning that go against the knowledge of God. Strongholds take root in the heart when we ignore God's teachings. That's why Paul instructed believers to wage war against strongholds and demolish every argument or thought that sets itself against the knowledge of God (2 Corinthians 10:4-5). While Paul spoke about false ideologies and taking the thoughts of others captive, perhaps this scripture can be applied to our own reasoning process. For instance, you can be a God-fearing, divorced, single, or married person, attend church regularly, serve in several ministries, and be used by God, and when you hear your preacher teach on tithing, you can still choose to not do it because

84

you think the church wants your money or because you have bills to pay.

When your preacher teaches on forgiving someone who hurt or upset you, you can find reasons or excuses not to forgive. You may justify your anger and decide to not speak to that person again unless they apologize, or maybe you decide to speak harshly to the person because of the offense. When you make these choices, a stronghold or firm grip has taken root in your heart, and the enemy can influence your thought life.

IN MY FEELINGS

When God gives instruction, we can follow our feelings, or we can follow His will. Naaman initially followed his feeling of anger when Elisha told him to go dip himself seven times in the Jordan river (2 Kings 5:10-11). The rich young ruler followed his feeling of disappointment when Jesus told him to sell all his possessions, give them to the poor to receive treasures in heaven, and then follow Him (Luke 18:22-23). I had to crucify my feeling of fear and the spirits of no and "I'm not doing it" in order to get healed and delivered from mistrust and rejection.

Life Lesson #9
Don't let your feelings or old habits drive your decisions over God's instruction.

Following instruction from God has been difficult at times. I don't always want to do what He instructs me to do even though, deep down, I know it will bring relief. I've struggled to let go of how I think, feel, and behave in order to follow His command. At times, I've chosen to wallow in excuses and self-pity instead of taking the necessary steps to get well. I've blamed the behavior of other people or my upbringing for why I behaved certain ways. But God has always given me a choice.

God's preference is for believers to choose life and live it to the fullest. His instruction brings life and my feelings brought death. Paul instructed believers to set the mind on the Spirit, which is life and peace, because to set it on the flesh brings death (Romans 8:6). Jesus needed to teach me a new way to see and overcome sorrow, betrayal, and disappointment from the death of my dreams, and choose the life He has in store for me.

I know so many women and men who struggle to let someone else gain access to their heart after experiencing betrayal and unspeakable hurt from parents, siblings, friends, and other family members. I also know women who won't allow other women to occupy space in their life because they believe the lie that all women are catty. Instead of following God's instruction to trust Him and let go, some people settle for maintaining walls, which blocks the path to the heart. Although God wants all believers to experience His perfect peace, particularly during difficult seasons, He will allow you to remain unchanged in your place of comfort.

Life Lesson #10
If your mind hasn't changed, the way that you act will remain the same.

CHAPTER 7
Season of Debt and Deliverance

*The LORD is my rock, my fortress and my deliverer; my God is my rock, in whom
I take refuge, my shield and the horn of my salvation, my stronghold.
(Psalm 18:2)*

TOTAL DEPENDENCE

When my marriage ended abruptly, it was hard for me to look at my life and have little to show for all those years. I. Was. Broke. I cried for days and nights after my separation, as I transitioned from being a married woman with two incomes, living in a 3500-square-foot, five-bedroom, five-bathroom home, to a single mother supporting a family of three, living in an 1,800-square-foot, three-bedroom apartment. I had massive amounts of debt, no emergency fund, and negative net worth. While I knew God was with me, I panicked at the thought of how I would financially take care of my young children. There were times when my rent, utilities, car note, food, student loan and credit card payments exceeded my monthly income, so I found myself living off my credit cards.

Soon, most of my credit cards were maxed out from purchasing food, gas, utilities, clothes, and whatever else we needed, and sometimes what we wanted. When my credit card bills were due, I made the minimum payment, waited for the payment to clear, and then charged the amount I'd just paid. It was a common practice for me to call the number on the back of each credit card to check to see how much room I had before I made a purchase. On one occasion, I used one credit card to charge $30 for gas, because that was all that I had left on it, and then I used another to charge $40 to finish filling up my tank. Other times, when I didn't have room left on my credit cards or money in the bank, the kids and I stayed home from work and school until my next pay day.

Added to my grief, I had accumulated over $1.1 million dollars in debt with zero assets and no money in the bank. I had over $80,000 in credit card debt, more than $300,000 in student loan debt, my bank account was overdrawn by $1000 on a monthly basis, I had a $550,000 home mortgage, $24,000 for home insurance, $40,000 car loan, private school tuition of $24,000 a year for two kids, and the list goes on. Added to this, the IRS was trying to garnish my wages due to $100,000 in unpaid taxes. I also had to deal with being sued by a construction company for $30,000 for breach of contract and unpaid wages for work done on my home.

My life felt like it was spiraling out of control. Given the enormity of my debt, I thought there was no way out of my situation. Even if I paid down some of my credit card debt, my student loan and IRS payments were still sky-high. The minimum payment on my student loan was $1800, which I couldn't afford, and the IRS wanted to take a chunk of my monthly salary to pay towards what was owed. While I knew God never left my side, boy, I wasn't sure how much stress and pressure my mind could take.

I'm sure you're wondering how I accumulated so much debt. In short, my husband and I made horrible financial choices. We purchased a $550,000 home that we couldn't afford (which we later short sold) and spent too much on improvements and repairs, chose to spend a ridiculous amount of money on new luxury vehicles that depreciated in value as soon as we drove them off the car lot, paid a full-time babysitter when our kids were young to watch them for eight hours a day while we worked, and later enrolled our kids in private school. We also had bad money habits, such as spending frivolously on clothes, dining out regularly, not tracking what we spent each month, and borrowing money.

If I'm being completely honest, I hadn't realized I'd accumulated so much debt during my marriage. Again, I'm sure you're reading this wondering how in the world did I not know how much debt I carried. Well, I was so engrossed and overwhelmed with paying my monthly expenses, dealing with responsibilities of motherhood, coming to the reality that my marriage was in trouble, managing my work demands, and the list goes on, that I didn't realize my debt had exploded. It's like weight gain. You know when you've picked up a few pounds, but you never know how much you've gained until you get on a scale. Until that happens, you can ignore your increasing weight even though your favorite pair of jeans fit more snugly. And then, one day you jump on the scale and discover you weigh more than you have in your entire life. Rather than making changes to lose weight, like regularly going to the gym and watching what you eat, you find yourself at another drive-thru, ordering a double-double burger, fries, and a large drink for dinner and then a sausage McMuffin with cheese and no egg the next morning. This pattern continues until you wake up one day and can't stand it any longer or maybe a doctor tells you your cholesterol and blood pressure are too high or you're prediabetic.

I had dug a financial hole for myself with no foreseeable way out. Not until I started spending time in the presence of God was I led to make changes in the area of my finances. God helped me realize paying off my debt was possible. But before He could bring financial deliverance and change the way I viewed money and debt, I needed to understand my total debt situation.

Life Lesson # 11
You can't pay off debt if you don't know how much you owe.

DEBT WOES

Carrying so much debt made single motherhood difficult. My phone rang off the hook with lenders and creditors who wanted to talk about when I planned to pay them. But all I could think about was feeding my children and keeping a roof over their heads. I was tempted to stop answering my phone and opening my mail, but I didn't have the luxury of completely falling apart. I had to shift gears into survival mode.

Once the kids and I settled into our new apartment, I quickly took inventory of my debt and attempted to cut expenses. For instance, I shopped at discount grocery stores and cut coupons to save money. When I was married, I didn't have to worry about penny-pinching on groceries. My husband and I purchased food when we needed it. But when I was single, my entire income needed to take care of three people and I could only spend a certain amount of money per month on food. I stocked up on beans, pasta, rice, and potatoes, as well as meats and vegetables, because those foods would stretch. But there were times when what I had wasn't enough. Every night, I waited for my children to eat first, and if there were leftovers, I too ate dinner.

As the price of regular unleaded gas rose to $4.99 a gallon, I drove to several gas stations to find cheap fuel. I also called all my credit card companies to see if I could get lower interest rates and an increase in my line of credit. My credit card with the highest interest rate was 21.99%. My minimum monthly payment on that credit card was $239 per month. Only one credit card company was willing to lower my interest rate if I agreed to close the account, which I did. After I exhausted those options, I looked at my highest expenses and urgent matters, which included IRS debt, private school tuition, and a car loan, to determine how to shave down cost.

IRS PURSUITS

When the IRS comes after you for unpaid taxes, you know you're in big trouble. When I first received the notice stating I owed more than $100,000 in back taxes, I almost lost it. Surely this was a typo. A mistake perhaps. I've always paid my taxes on time. But when I called, the person on the other end of the phone confirmed it was true. He told me my husband and I hadn't filed taxes in three years. When taxes aren't filed, the IRS estimates what they believe you owe. There was no way in the world I could pay back $100,000 even if they put me on a payment plan.

Filing joint returns for three years would require cooperation from my husband, but it was difficult to contact him at times. He was inconsistent with returning phone calls and text messages. Plus, I knew I'd need to collect his W-2's for three years and scrape up money to file our taxes. While all this danced around in my mind, I received a notice from my employer that the IRS planned to levy my wages. As a state employee, it was easier for them to pursue wage garnishment against me. I disclosed what was happening (my debt and divorce) in my life to the payroll department at my job, which was humiliating. While no one from the department could prevent my wages from being garnished, I felt compelled to explain my dilemma because I didn't want them to think I was irresponsible.

Each pay period, I was again on the phone with the IRS. I cannot tell you the number of people I spoke with at the IRS to plead my case. For starters, I repeatedly stressed I didn't know we owed over $100,000 in back taxes. I also told them my husband and I were separated and I had two small children to support on my income. The IRS was only pursuing me, not my husband because it was easier to locate an employee of the State whereas a person who moved jobs frequently. It felt as if everything was collapsing in my life all at once.

When I shared with my husband what was happening, he told me to keep him posted with no panic or concern in his voice. I was completely dumbfounded. Here I was, trying to convince a government agency not to totally disrupt my life while at the same time figuring out how the heck I'd pay $100,000 without my husband's support. I was frantic. I was looking for my husband to weigh in and help me develop a strategy to pay the IRS, particularly because it was joint debt, but he never did.

During the marriage, my husband oversaw our taxes. He found the person we worked with and scheduled the appointments. One year, he told me he didn't want to pay someone to prepare our taxes when we would still owe the IRS money. I didn't realize he stopped filing our taxes from that point on.

Within a month or so, my husband and I were assigned a tax advocate, assigned to taxpayers having difficulty resolving problems with the IRS, to help us resolve our debt challenges. It was incredibly helpful. My tax advocate made several attempts to reach out to my husband with no success, so she decided to work exclusively with me. She informed me I could request innocent spouse relief, which in short, granted me relief from taxes owed from the time we were married.

My husband was furious when he learned he was dropped as a client by the tax advocate. He was upset with me for not convincing her to keep him as a client even though he never returned any of her calls. He told me he was too busy and thought I was handling everything. I wasn't sure how his inability to file our taxes, his choice in not returning the calls from the tax advocate, and his loss of representation were all my fault.

Again, I went to God in prayer for help. I didn't know what to do, but I knew God would bring me an answer to my problems. One day after praying, I watched one of Joyce Meyer's teachings, and she told her viewers, "We have not, because we ask not." She stressed the importance of boldly going to God and asking for whatever you need.

She quoted John 15:7, "If you remain in me and my words remain in you, ask whatever you wish, and it will be done for you." Joyce shared the story of when she needed dishrags for her kitchen and didn't have enough money to purchase them. She prayed and asked God for dishrags, and a neighbor bought her new dishrags as a gift.

Life Lesson #12
Be bold and ask God for what you need.

I knew I abided in God and He abided in me, so I boldly prayed and asked Him for debt cancellation and forgiveness. Not just the $100,000 I owed to the IRS, but also the $550,000 of debt remaining after we did the short sale on our house. By His grace, I was granted relief from the $100,000 taxes owed during my marriage through various abatements, and a portion of the taxes were cancelled, which stopped the pursuits by the IRS. This was when I met God: Jehovah Jireh, the Lord My Provider.

It took eleven months of endless phone calls and countless prayers for God to bring forth not so much an answer as a lesson. He taught me what it means to totally depend on Him no matter what I encountered. For whatever reason, when there was trouble in my life, I had the habit of reaching out to my husband for help. I wanted him to step in, put his cape on, and save the day. I thought of him as a modern-day Superman. I wanted him to protect and shield me. But whenever I sought his sympathy, compassion, and willingness to step forth, I was disappointed and frustrated. God used my disappointment to show me He is my provider. He is the One who intercedes on my behalf, touches hearts, and connects me with those who have compassion and understanding.

Knowing the IRS was no longer pursuing me lifted a heavy burden from my shoulders. When they finally went after my husband, he called me to discuss what steps he should take. Here's where I wanted to tell him to keep me posted, but I didn't. Instead, I told him that he should consider making payment arrangements, which he chose not to do. Consequently, the IRS froze his banking accounts and took a sizable amount of money, which he called to tell me about. I'm sure he eventually worked out his IRS issues, but I had other matters that required my attention.

PRIVATE OR PUBLIC SCHOOL

My next step in lowering my monthly expenses was to remove my children from private school. Although I received some help from their father to pay the tuition, it was incredibly expensive. In the beginning, the tuition was $500 per month, and over the years it grew to $2200 per month. The required age to enroll in public school was five, and my son was only three. My daughter, on the other hand, was eligible to enroll in public school at the time, but I wanted to keep them in school together. The public school system in our new neighborhood also battled with low test scores, unqualified teachers, high suspension rates among African American students, and limited resources.

The private school was predominantly White and enjoyed plentiful resources. Although my husband initially absorbed most of the tuition cost, he soon told me he couldn't afford to keep paying it. However, during our marriage, we had agreed that keeping our kids in private school was incredibly important because of the poor quality of education in the nearby public schools. I panicked. I no longer lived in the city where my kids went to school. If I enrolled them in school in my new neighborhood, it would take me and hour and a half to get to them if they needed me or became sick.

I needed to do something, so I reached out to the director and head of the school to request a meeting. I was embarrassed to yet again explain what was happening in my life, but I did. I told them about my divorce, that I had moved to another city because the rents were cheaper, and I shared that, on my salary, I couldn't afford to pay the cost of tuition alone. The director offered me comfort and shared her divorce story. She also mentioned it was best to manage the affairs of my children independently particularly because it was obvious my husband was never present to help.

I was utterly mortified. I felt judged by her statement. While what she said was true, hearing her say it out loud and being aware that others saw my husband's lack of involvement was humiliating. Because the school was so small, his absence at events, activities, and parent-teacher conferences was noticeable. It was bad enough I had to live this new reality.

During the meeting, I petitioned for a reduction in tuition. The director and head of school needed to take my request to the board of directors, and they said they would let me know the outcome. I was afraid for so many reasons. First, I thought the other parents would judge me. I was certain news traveled fast in our small school community. By the end of the week, most of the families would know I needed financial support and my husband had left me. I wasn't sure which was worse, people knowing I could no longer afford to send my children to private school or the shame I felt because my husband repeatedly cheated on me and finally left. In any event, both weighed heavy on my heart.

Second, I was afraid my request would be denied because I wasn't actively involved in the school and didn't put in all my required volunteer hours. When you enroll your kids in private school, parents are often required to participate on committees, in activities, or in the classroom. At our kids' school, if parents didn't volunteer fifty hours per parent, we were assessed $500 each. Given that my husband no longer attended any of the events and never volunteered, I'd have to absorb the entire cost. I didn't have time to serve on committees or attend field trips during my work hours.

I went to God in prayer and asked Him to touch hearts and intercede on my behalf regarding my request for tuition assistance. He again answered my prayers. I was so thankful to receive tuition relief. Instead of paying $1100 per child, the tuition cost dropped to $500 per child, plus the cost of aftercare.

Fortunately, my husband was willing to help with the lower amount, but he still insisted I needed to investigate other options for schooling. He suggested I consider moving closer to his mother, where the public schools were highly ranked. While that sounded fantastic, his mother lived in one of the most expensive cities in the Bay Area. The cost to rent a one-bedroom apartment was more than I could afford. And renting someone's house was out of the question.

Rather than give serious consideration to his suggestion, I prayed and felt at peace keeping my kids in private school for another year until God showed me my next move.

FROM LEASE TO LOAN

My next step to lower my monthly expenses was to finance my leased car. I strongly recommend against leasing any vehicle, but it was one of the many bad decisions I'd made in my finances. With a lease, you never own the vehicle, you're limited in the number of miles you can drive, you'll be charged for wear and tear on the car, and the cost to purchase the vehicle at the end of the lease is always higher than it would be if you bought the same car. I really wanted to purchase the Lexus R330 because its high safety ranking and because I had issues with my lower back. When we were together, my husband and I went to the dealership to determine what type of finance deal I could get with my credit. My husband suggested I lease the vehicle and recommended I turn in the lease after three-years and purchase something else.

96

Five-years down the road, I still had the leased car, but after my husband left, it was time for me to turn it in. Normally, he would have negotiated the terms and conditions for my car since women often are taken advantage of when they try to purchase a car. I was completely ignorant of the process, but given my husband's unwillingness to participate in helping with the IRS, it was a safe bet he wouldn't feel benevolent and choose to help me.

When it was time to turn in my lease, I thought it would be easier to buy the same car instead of listening to someone give me a sales pitch and take advantage of my ignorance. Purchasing the lease meant I needed to finance the car. Yet again, another colossal mistake. By the time I left the dealership, my interest rate was over ten percent, which I agreed to in order to avoid paying penalties on the lease. The good news was my car payments dropped from $800 per month to $650. On one hand, I was happy my car note went down by $150, but I was also unhappy with the rate. Negotiating a lower finance rate wasn't my area of expertise. I simply did not educate myself enough before I went into the dealership.

My best friend had recently joined a credit union and suggested I try to refinance through them. She gave me all the information I needed, and I signed up with the same credit union with hopes of refinancing my vehicle. However, when I submitted my vehicle refinance application, I was denied. My debt-to-income ratio was high, and my credit score had tanked over the years. So I waited six months, applied again, and was approved. My monthly car payment dropped from $650 to $380 a month with a 2.9 percent interest rate. On the positive side, my monthly expenses were lowered, but on the negative side, I drove the same vehicle for ten years and still owed $6,000 when I later traded it in.

Through the credit union, I also applied for a personal loan, so I could consolidate some of my credit card debt. Fortunately, I was approved for $15,000, which allowed me to consolidate four of my twelve credit cards. Yes, twelve credit cards! While four may seem insignificant, given the total number of cards I possessed, my monthly payments on those credit cards dropped from $575 a month to $300. My interest rate on the personal loan was 6.9 percent. As I mentioned earlier, my credit card debt was $80,000, and some relief was better than no relief at all.

> *Key Thought:*
> *Debt is not meant to crush you, but to move you into a season of total dependence on God.*

GOD TURNS THE ILLUSION OF CHAOS INTO A PERFECT PLAN

God moved forcibly in my life and helped me eliminate more than $651,300 of debt in a short time frame. Over the next six years, I prayed God would bring me financial increase, relief, and debt cancellation with my remaining debt. I wanted Him to supernaturally eliminate all my debt, so I could start my life over as a single mother with zero debt, which I thought would be the perfect solution. An alternative solution was for God to increase my finances through a job opportunity, which would allow me to pay off my debt. I even debated if I should pursue filing for bankruptcy. But God had a different plan in mind. "'For I know the plans I have for you,'" declares the LORD, 'plans to prosper and not to harm you, plans to give you hope and a future'" (Jeremiah 29:11). God's plans are impeccable. While we cannot see His hand at work in all areas of our life, He sees our story from the beginning to the end.

God could have eliminated all my debt, but I believe His plan was to teach me how to develop better financial habits and bring peace into this area of my life. But how? Why did it take several years for God to teach me how to change my poor financial habits? Why didn't God move swiftly like he did earlier, particularly since He knew I was desperate for my situation to change? Perhaps the answer is best illustrated in the book of Exodus. When God delivered the Israelites from years of oppression by the Egyptians, He led them down an unexpected route. The Bible states, "When Pharaoh let the people go, God did not lead them on the road through the Philistine country, though that was shorter. For God said, 'If they face war, they might change their minds and return to Egypt'" (Exodus 13:17).

God purposely led the Israelites around the desert because He knew they would return to their bondage in Egypt if they encountered war. Similarly, God knew if He supernaturally delivered me from my debt, I would return to my old patterns of spending, charging everything on credit cards, not saving money, and not planning for my future. God also knew I wasn't ready to do what was required to get out of debt, which meant budgeting and planning to pay off debt. By faith, I believed God would help me, but I had to do my part to pay off my remaining debt. However, my separation left me in a state of emergency, so I didn't take a course of action based on long-term planning.

EXCUSES ARE THE TOOLS OF THE INCOMPETENT

One day, I was praying for debt relief again and was struck by the story in the Bible about a paralyzed man (John 5:1-15). The short version of the story is that Jesus was headed to a festival in Jerusalem and came upon a pool where the lame, blind, and paralyzed gathered. When Jesus saw a man, who had been paralyzed for thirty-eight years, Jesus asked him, "Do you want to get well?" Rather than say, "Absolutely Jesus, I want to get well," the man made excuses for why he couldn't get well. Jesus finally told the man, "Get up! Pick up your mat and walk!"

Like the paralyzed man, I had been in debt for more than twenty years and made excuses for why I remained so. I told myself I was in debt because the cost of living in the San Francisco Bay Area was high and my salary wasn't enough. I also thought debt was normal. Given my high student loan and credit card debt, I believed I'd be in debt for the rest of my life. Although some of what I thought was true—the cost of living was incredibly high in the Bay Area and my income wasn't as competitive as I wanted—I accumulated the bulk of my debt due to poor decision-making.

My prayers centered on debt forgiveness, cancellation, and relief, but God revealed to me I was in debt because I didn't do the work to get myself out. God provided me with income from my job, but I needed to take stock of how much debt I had, develop a plan, establish a budget, stop charging on my credit cards, and commit to paying off debt.

Life Lesson #13
It's not about how much money you make, but how you manage what you make.

Back in college, when I sought initiation into my sorority, I, along with others were told, "Excuses are the tools of the incompetent, they build monuments of nothingness, and those who dwell upon them are seldom less than anything else, EXCUSES!" No matter how rational my thoughts were, I made excuses as to why I remained in debt. There was no point debating with God or anyone else whether I was making excuses or had reasonable explanations for the choices I'd made.

At the end of the day, I still had debt I needed to pay off. God knew I had to grow, mature, and stop making excuses for why I was in debt and relinquish the bad habits and mindsets that landed me there.

Life Lesson #14
God won't transform your bad habits into better habit if you're unwilling to let Him.

100

FINANCIAL PEACE

After God brought me revelation about my bad financial choices, habits, and excuses, I still needed help. I needed a strategy. And God is in the business of giving believers strategies. Joseph gave Pharaoh a strategy from God to deal with the years of abundance and famine. God gave Joshua and David a strategy to defeat their enemies and lead His people.

I shared my debt dilemma with a friend who had successfully paid off her credit card and home loan debt. She did this on her retirement income. I was telling myself and others I couldn't get out of debt on my salary, and God introduced me to a woman who made less money and still paid off her house. I cannot tell you the number of times I heard of people who paid off their debt and I said, "Well, yeah, it must have been easier for that person because" or "When I make more money, I can do that."

God purposefully brought someone into my life who was a divorced, single mother, made less income, and paid off a large sum of debt, so I wouldn't make excuses as to why I couldn't do the same thing. He knew I needed a real-life example. She too had responsibilities of raising a child and providing. She desired to travel and pursue additional schooling, but she made the choice to pay off debt and save for whatever she wanted or needed.

That same woman sent me *The Money Makeover*, by Dave Ramsey, and told me she followed his plan to help her live debt-free. All I can say is the testimonies and strategies in Dave Ramsey's book were eye-opening, proven, and effective. Based on my reading, I established an emergency fund, developed a budget, and listed all my debts from smallest to large. Within a year and a half, I paid off all my credit card debt. Hallelujah! Thank you, Jesus! This year, I'm on target to pay off my car loan, and then move on to paying off my student loans.

I didn't realize this woman and the book she gifted me with were part of the answer to my prayers for debt relief. But there was more to God's plan. He revealed to me that living debt-free and experiencing financial wholeness and peace isn't always about implementing a quick ten-point plan, using the snowball or avalanche methodology, or completing a course on financial freedom. While all four approaches are effective in increasing the likelihood of debt freedom, there are some things only the Holy Spirit can fix because He truly knows me.

I could use whatever methodology I wanted to become debt-free, but it wouldn't mean anything if my mind remained in bondage. I know several people who have paid off all their debt at different points, only to repeat the same behaviors time and time again because their thoughts were not transformed. Ask God to teach you the strategies to pay off your debt and live in His peace concerning your finances.

Life Lesson #15
You can live debt-free without experiencing financial peace.

For me, financial peace wasn't about living debt-free. It was letting God un-train my mind regarding my finances, so I could walk and live in His peace. Remember God's will is for believers to not be slaves to debt (Proverbs 22:7) and God's peace isn't based on circumstances (John 16:33). Therefore, I needed God to examine and transform my thoughts, which was the other part of His plan to bring me financial peace.

I didn't want to go through all Dave Ramsey's baby steps to get debt-free, only to find myself back in debt years down the road because of unresolved behaviors that were a result of psychological, emotional, or spiritual scarring. Psalm 139:1-4 is full of godly wisdom and the key to unlocking financial peace:

You have searched me, LORD, and you know me. You know when I sit and when I rise; you perceive my thoughts from afar. You discern my going out and my lying down; you are familiar with all my ways. Before a word is on my tongue you, LORD, know it completely.

This scripture reveals God *knows* you and me. I used pretense to hide parts of myself from people. No one could see the root cause of why I landed in debt; they only saw the symptoms. The symptoms (maxed out credit cards, undisciplined spending, eating out too often, expensive car purchase, etc.) were indicators of my debt-forming behaviors. For me, following the snowball methodology described in Dave Ramsey's book temporarily treated my symptoms, but it also masked my real problem.

Only the Holy Spirit could uncover the root cause of my debt behaviors. He looked beyond my behaviors and saw deeper into my problem. The passage above highlights that there is no hiding from God because He knows me and what I think and is familiar with *all* my ways. God knew where my thoughts about money and debt originated and how to deliver me from financial bondage to peace.

Life Lesson #16
God can't fix anything when you choose to not take responsibility for your actions.

The Lord revealed that addressing the root cause of my debt behaviors required action on my part.

Step 1: Consider my ways.

Think about how God spoke through Haggai (Haggai 1:5-11) to the children of Israel, telling them to consider their ways. God commanded the people to rebuild His temple, but they procrastinated.

They left what He called them to do unattended. God essentially told them to give thought to their ways, to reflect and evaluate. This same principle applied to my debt dilemma. Although I went to God on many occasions concerning my debt, as I mentioned before, I didn't consider the behaviors that landed me in debt. I wanted God to fix the situation by providing a miracle without my taking responsibility for my past behaviors.

Not surprisingly, the way I spent money was directly tied to my heart. Scripture teaches that the heart is deceitful (Jeremiah 17:9), and where our treasure is, there our heart will be also (Matthew 6:21). God showed me I treasured the image I projected to others, which resulted in impulsive spending. He revealed that my heart wasn't in the kingdom of God because my treasure was in people and things. More specifically, my love for what other people thought about my lifestyle and the things of this world contributed to my financial state. These behaviors stemmed for growing up believing I lacked certain material possessions, so I overcompensated by purchasing things to mask feelings of inadequacy and inferiority.

STEP 2: Be a good steward.

In the story of the talents (Matthews 25:14-30), a business owner went out of town and entrusted his money to three of his employees. Upon his return, he met with each employee to evaluate what they did with his money and rewarded them according to how well they managed his wealth. To the two employees who invested his money and made a profit, the business owner said, "Well done, good and faithful servant. You have been faithful over a little; I will set you over much. Enter into the joy of your master." The other employee, who did not invest his employer's money and instead hid it, was called wicked.

104

This parable is often used in sermons to illustrate how believers should steward over the talents and gifts bestowed on them by God. However, there's a financial principle on trustworthiness and responsibility in the parable as well. In my case, I couldn't be trusted with managing the money God provided, yet I was praying He would bless me with additional income. Scripture states, "So if you have not been trustworthy in handling worldly wealth, who will trust you with true riches?" (Luke 16:11).

God also knew I wasn't ready to handle the additional responsibility that went along with increased compensation. He had watched me over the years to test how I spent my money, and He knew my hidden motive for wanting more money went beyond my desire to provide a comfortable lifestyle for my children. The truth was I wanted to satisfy my spirit of lust for things to prove to myself and others that I wasn't a failure.

Step 3: Discipline yourself.

I couldn't experience spiritual wholeness, living well in spirit and mind, without help from the Holy Spirit. What does this mean? I lacked spiritual discipline. I choose the word spiritual discipline rather than the word self-discipline on purpose. While both requires the ability to control one's behavior or conduct, spiritual discipline requires the work of the Holy Spirit to help you control debt triggers and temptations in your life, including spending money unwisely. I do believe, however, that self-discipline is necessary and can get many of us to a certain point, but I also believe that spiritual discipline will help us *overcome* our debt forming habits and enter into the fullness of God. Consider asking God to search your heart for those known and unknown emotional or psychological factors that interfere with experiencing financial peace.

Step 4: Think long term, not short term.

I needed help from the Lord to shift my focus from short-term thinking to long-term thinking. My mind was trained by the culture of instant gratification, to think here and now and paycheck to paycheck, although that's not how I was raised to think. I had a mindset of "you only live once" (YOLO), which was short-term thinking. But God showed me I couldn't indulge in short-term thinking because it was shortsighted. He revealed that quick-fix approaches and behaviors were not His will. For instance, I wanted a huge settlement, bonus, or tax refund to wipe out all my debt. The Lord knew I wanted another easy escape without taking full ownership of the debt I accumulated. But He also knew I needed to commit to getting spiritually well and engaging in long-term solutions, otherwise I would return to Egypt, my place of financial bondage.

Step 5: Pursue financial peace.

John 14:27 says, "Peace I leave with you; my peace I give you. I do not give to you as the world gives. Do not let your hearts be troubled and do not be afraid." This is a wonderful promise given to believers from Jesus. The peace offered by the world is based on your circumstances. For instance, when your bills are paid, debt is low or gone, and you have money stashed in your savings account, the world will tell you that you're at peace. But the peace of God has nothing to do with our circumstances. His peace surpasses all understanding and guards our heart and mind in Christ Jesus (Philippians 4:7). The peace of God is a gift which comes from our relationship with Jesus, and something that we, as believers are called to pursue. You can have peace from God even if you're in debt up the wazoo.

Getting to the root cause of my debt problem took time. The Lord revealed what I'm sharing with you over a period of six years, and He is still working, unfolding, and delivering me from bad habits. There were psychological reasons for why I was in debt, which connected to my emotional habits. I had certain proclivities God needed to purge. But once He revealed what they were, I fought debt in the spiritual realm using keys lessons described in this book, which led me to experiencing financial peace.

CHAPTER 8
Season of Singleness

But seek first his kingdom and his righteousness, and all these things will be given to you as well.
(Matthews 6:33)

SOUL TIES

Dating someone is an emotional process and should not be taken lightly, especially after you've experienced trauma and hurt. The dating process can cause connections best described as "soul ties," your mind and body are spiritually attached. Although not explicitly discussed in Scripture, soul ties can be emotional, psychological, physical, romantic, or all the above. Romantic soul ties are not always physical but can create the sensation of feeling of being swept off your feet and caught in a whirlwind of euphoric feelings.

Some soul ties are healthy and will lift you spiritually, however, some are unhealthy and dangerous. Whether your dating relationship is physical or not, certain emotional connections can contaminate your soul. It can cause invisible wounds, like open cuts that never completely heal without help from the Lord. Simply put, soul ties in dating can either be wonderful or hinder your spiritual growth.

The moment you begin giving your time and energy to another person, emotional attachments start to form. The more interactions you have, in which both parties share their thoughts, desires, hopes, dreams, and challenges, the greater the emotional entanglements. Once the physical and/or emotional bond is established, you can become consumed, ignoring intuitions and overreacting to situations, making it tough to recover or process pain or other or put an end to the relationship when necessary.

After my husband left, I stayed in God's presence for three years, learning, growing, and becoming. By this time, I wanted to start dating, but soon discovered I still had wounds that weren't quite healed. Selfishly, my desire to date came from my interest to feel wanted by a man and to regain the security I'd lost. I loved the idea of romantic gestures and encounters. The thought of kind words, holding hands, receiving a gentle yet firm hug, and having someone ask me about my day made my heart yearn for closeness. These desires pushed me forward without fully realizing my choices weren't aligned with God's will for my life.

I remember when I finally decided to date someone, who I'll call Johnny, several years after my husband left. After talking to each other on the phone for hours, texting, and spending time together for seven months, we developed an emotional connection. The more we talked, the deeper the connection grew. I started to cleave to him because he was attentive, supportive, and responsive. These traits resonated with me after having experienced unresponsiveness and emotional distance in my marriage.

I enjoyed the consistency of his calls, commitment level, and concern for me and my children. I dated him because he was safe; someone who wouldn't purposefully hurt me. I knew Johnny loved me because he often told me, but I didn't love him in the same way. I liked his companionship and the idea of dating more than I liked him. Added to this difference in feelings, I never considered a future with him.

Johnny possessed so many wonderful attributes, but when we had disagreements, I saw signs of immaturity and stubbornness in how he

110

handled conflict. I knew in my heart the relationship wouldn't last, but instead of releasing him, I selfishly held on to the security and friendship he offered.

One night, Dayshawnna called to tell me her mother, Charlotte was in town and wanted to stop by and visit. It was close to eight o'clock. When they arrived, Charlotte explained she came to town to take care of a friend who was recovering from a double mastectomy, but she realized God actually sent her to the Bay Area to bring me a word from Him.

The Lord wanted her to convey at least a dozen things. For starters, He wanted me to know the man I was dating, Johnny, was not the person He had for me. Let's pause. Neither Dayshawnna nor I ever told her I was dating. Only Dayshawnna and another close friend knew about Johnny. Charlotte went on to say the person the Lord had for me was tall, would fly in and look for me, have a ministry, and partner with me in my purpose.

She proceeded to tell me the man I was dating played with God's name. I knew exactly what she meant. On several occasions, I noticed Johnny would say, "Thank God." And each time, I knew in my spirit he said those words for my benefit and not because he was thankful to God. Perhaps it was Johnny's way of trying to connect with me. At first, I told myself my love for God was rubbing off on him. But that wasn't true.

She also told me because I was dating this man I was no longer under God's protective hedge. Okay, so this scared the bejesus out of me. The gravity of her words and the realization of my actions sat in the pit of my stomach. God places a protective wall around believers like a spiritual fortress. It's the most sacred and safest place to be as a child of God. After my husband left, I enjoyed God's peace, comfort, provision, and protection. It held me together when everything around me was falling apart, and here I was, jeopardizing everything because of another wrong choice.

If God chooses, He can lower His protective hedge or shield, as He did with Job, not to punish, but to show us the misfortune we'll face without Him. We can also move from under God's hedge of grace when we engage in willful sin. God didn't remove His protection; I left it.

With a serious expression on her face, she told me to get back under God's protection by repenting, to turn away or stop engaging in sin. She also said to end the relationship and that it wouldn't be as difficult as I thought. For weeks, before Charlotte told me what the Lord said, I mulled over calling off the relationship, but I didn't do it because I thought it would be emotionally challenging. I didn't want to go through another breakup. Instead, I remained and stayed yoked to an unbeliever. My emotional attachment caused me to ignore God's will. The Bible is clear: I must not yoke myself with an unbeliever. In essence, I knowingly disobeyed God's instruction. Needless to say, within a day, I broke off the relationship, and it wasn't as hard as I thought. While Johnny was upset, I felt a huge sense of relief because I obeyed God and repositioned myself under His protective hedge.

There was another issue with dating Johnny. I was still legally married. I naively thought that it was okay to date as long as I was living apart from my husband. We had been separated for three years, but I didn't have the emotional bandwidth to deal with the divorce process. It wasn't a priority, not because I thought reconciliation was in our future, but because the process was a huge hassle.

One Sunday, I attended church, and I heard my pastor say if you're not divorced, you should not be dating because you're leading the person you're dating into sin. He went on to tell the congregation too many believers enter into relationships, knowing they haven't even started their divorce paperwork. Yep, that was me. The pastor asked, "How can God bring you someone to marry when you're still in covenant with someone else?" Then he yelled, "Finish your paperwork!" I heard the Lord's message loud and clear and finalized my divorce within several months.

The prophecy I received from the Lord was so thorough. God also spoke about Johnny's financial standing and lack of motivation, but He knew and understood why I was dating Johnny and was patient with me. The other things the Lord told Charlotte to share were unrelated to dating but were about my future purpose, family, and husband.

Have you ever received a prophetic word from the Lord that brought you to your knees? I felt His gaze upon me when Charlotte spoke on His behalf. His words burrowed into my spirit. I once heard a pastor say God will always bring His people a word of correction before destruction. I was unknowingly destroying my purpose by dating Johnny, and thankfully, the Lord stepped in the middle of my mess and held up a spiritual stop sign.

Receiving a word of correction from someone is a gift from God. He cares so much about choices believers make and wants us to change the direction when we're headed the wrong way. His correction is meant to lead us to repentance and Truth. And as difficult as it may be, we need to embrace correction from God, for He knows what's ahead. Keep in mind there's much more spiritually at stake than we realize.

Since then, I've dated two other men and formed emotional attachments with both. One struggled with whether to follow God or the world's value system, and over time, the relationship became emotionally exhausting and spiritually draining. The Lord quickened my spirit about letting him go as well, which was a huge relief. Four years later, I dated the third man, who I'll call Isaac, and he had a relationship with God. We had similar values and beliefs. We got along well and connected beautifully. He was thoughtful, kind, principled, and honest. He was respectful of others, passionate about serving students, and had a ministry of mentoring teenage boys.

Isaac and I connected on every level. Post-divorce, he was the first man with whom I saw a glimmer of hope that he might be "the one." He pursued me relentlessly. We invested so much time in our connection with one another. He never had difficulty expressing his thoughts and communicated transparently what was in his heart, and I was an open book. We seemed to speak each other's love languages. The only problem was that he was separated from his wife. And here I go again!

Isaac started his divorce proceedings. There's nothing wrong with that, right? And here's where the devil convinced me, for a few months, that it was acceptable to date someone as long as they'd already *started* the divorce process. Satan will always try to convince you what you're doing is not a sin. You might hear something in your head like "It's not a big deal. At least he already started his paperwork." If you recall, my ex-husband filed for divorce eight months or so after he left, meaning he started the process. But it wasn't until I gathered the required documents, crafted the marital settlement agreement, retrieved his signature, had the documents notarized, paid the court fees, filed the documents with the court, and received the dissolution of marriage from the courts that my marriage was dissolved.

Marriage is a covenant with God. The marital covenant ends when the couple legally divorces and not when they start the paperwork. And as much as I loved Isaac, the fact was his divorce was not final. I went to God in prayer for guidance. And the word that I received strongly in my spirit were "do not covet." Not only were those words in my spirit, when I opened my Bible after I prayed, it just so happened I landed on Romans 13:8-10, which reads,

Let no debt remain outstanding, except the
continuing debt to love one another, for whoever
loves others has fulfilled the law.

114

The commandments, "You shall not commit adultery,"
"You shall not murder," "You shall not steal,"
"You shall not covet," and whatever other command there may be,
are summed up in this one command:
"Love your neighbor as yourself."
Love does no harm to a neighbor.
Therefore love is the fulfillment of the law.

I was distraught, having heard from the Lord, because a soul tie had already formed. I didn't want to let Isaac go, especially because I thought he was the one for me. Isaac also wanted to continue our relationship while simultaneously finishing his paperwork. We were both torn because we'd talked about getting married. Before you jump to conclusions, Isaac's decision to separate from his marriage predated me, but in retrospect, we should have waited to date one another until his divorce was finalized.

And like before, Charlotte gave me a prophetic word from God. Without knowing the details of my relationship, she told me that, a few days before we spoke, God had given her the word release. She wasn't sure what it meant, so she went back to Him in prayer for two days and still heard Him say the word release. When I told her about aspects of my relationship with Isaac, she knew exactly what God wanted her to say. She softly told me the Lord wanted me to release Isaac, not back to his marriage, but to Him. Isaac also had a calling on his life and a purpose, and if I didn't release him so he could return to God's presence, he wouldn't awaken to his purpose.

I didn't want to release Isaac. I thought he was part of God's plan for my life, and I was heartbroken. But Charlotte told me to trust God. As badly as I wanted to continue with the relationship and as heartbroken I felt, Isaac and I parted ways.

I saw him a year later at a conference. He mentioned he was there in hopes of seeing me, so he could apologize for starting a relationship with me while he was still married. Who does that? Who extends an unsolicited apology for something they did wrong? He did. He said he wanted to do what was right. Even though it was difficult to see and speak with him, we greeted one another warmly and again said our goodbyes. Five years have passed since my breakup with Isaac, and we haven't seen or spoken to one another since.

DETOX

Remember you are made up of the flesh, soul, and spirit. The soul is the mind, will, and emotions. The spirit is the Holy Spirit. When your soul, your flesh (or both) becomes attached to someone during dating, so does God's spirit. When you break up with someone, you need God's help to cleanse you from the inside out and surgically sever the soul ties because your flesh, soul, and spirit were interconnected (Hebrews 4:12).

Keep in mind that the process to sever soul ties is painful because two souls were spiritually joined together. The separation involved produces grief. And when the separation becomes hard to bear, the temptation is to run back to the person, return their calls or text messages, convince yourself you cannot live without the person, or tell yourself you're tired of being alone. Whatever the case, you'll need to decide whether to trust God and release the relationship in your heart to Him, so He can heal you, or return to a spiritually destructive bond.

Emotional Detox

Emotions can be tricky, particularly in the context of dating. You typically experience a range of emotions, such as love, happiness, trust, and acceptance. But when the relationship ends after your spirit has become emotionally, psychologically, romantically, and/or physically intertwined with someone, you may find ourselves dwelling

116

VERNELL DESLONDE

on the complexities of our emotions. And like you purge the body of impurities through a cleansing process, the Holy Spirit is needed to help you as a believer to free yourself of ungodly attachments by detoxing. This is especially necessary if your relationship was abusive or filled with strife, anger, bitterness, or grief because soul ties are subtle and hard to detect and linger long after the relationship has ended.

The point of an emotional detox isn't to eliminate all the hurt and pain that happened while you dated because there's value, meaning, and lessons learned from your mistakes and pain. There's also personal and spiritual growth that comes from distress. This book was birthed from my hurt and pain because of an ungodly soul tie. The idea is to let God help you process those feelings, recalibrate, and sever those ungodly connections. I recognize, however, that while dating, many people experience trauma that may stem from early childhood experiences. And if the pain cuts deep and the suffering was severe, a therapy detox may also be in order.

The other point of an emotional detox is to pour out all the emotions that you have bottled up inside. This process allows believers to examine and cleanse out toxic thoughts, feelings, and behaviors that were revealed from the relationships.

After my relationship with Isaac ended, my emotions were all over the place. Residual feelings lingered, and I found myself thinking about our conversations and reminiscing about the times we spent together and the dreams we shared. I heard songs, smelled fragrances, and passed places that reminded me of him. I felt sad because there was loss involved and the death of another dream. Because I loved Isaac and our spirits were attached, I thought of him years after the relationship ended. I wondered how he was doing, whether he was happy, and whether we'd ever see each other again. I thought of what a future with him would look like, and I wondered how frequently he thought of me.

117

My memories of Isaac infiltrated every area of my life. He was in my dreams and the deep recesses of my heart. If Isaac had walked back into my life at that time and was divorced, I would have taken him back in a heartbeat. My soul-tie ran deep. To sever the connection, I needed God to help me rein in my thoughts and feelings and release my past, which occurred by using the three steps discussed in chapter five. I meditated on God's word, professed the Word over my life, and experienced God's peace as a way to process my feelings.

I'd love to say the act of meditating and professing God's word over my life led to instant peace and the reining in of my thoughts. It did not. No magic elixir can make grief disappear overnight. I cried my eyes out for weeks and, for more than a year, tried my best not to think about Isaac or the mistakes I made in my dating relationships. Through prayer, I asked God to help me release Isaac and move forward with my life. And amid my prayers, a year later, I relived my pain all over again when I saw him at a conference.

The thing about prayer is that you must pray without quitting. It's so tempting to quit praying and believe that, since emotional healing didn't happen overnight or you feel disappointed with God, you didn't get what you wanted. And on top of that feeling, you look on social media and seemingly everyone you know is happily living their best life with the person they love. That's when it's easy to become discouraged. However, when I looked back over the trauma and self-doubt, lack of self-worth, and insecurities I experienced from my divorce, I realized God had healed me before, and He would do it again. That realization kept my faith strong. My trust and faith in God kept me believing there was joy on the other side of my pain even when I felt emotionally depleted.

Prayer helped me process my feelings. Rather than run away from God and hide or delve deeper into my feelings and emotions, I stayed connected with Him through prayer, remained open to receiving words of correction, asked for forgiveness and healing, and repented. God knew I would make mistakes, particularly because my reasons for dating were selfish, which He understood and lovingly corrected.

Psalm 19:12-13 says,

> *But who can discern their own errors?*
> *Forgive my hidden faults.*
> *Keep your servant also from willful sins;*
> *may they not rule over me.*
> *Then I will be blameless,*
> *innocent of great transgression.*

This scripture is powerful and taught me there's nothing God cannot expose or forgive. This is why an active prayer life is important. My spirit was weakened from my soul ties, which produced behaviors contrary to God's word, and I needed to feed my spirit with His word.

Recalibration and Heart Detox

One would think I needed a heart detox because of the way my heart ached for Isaac after our relationship ended. But the real reason I needed the Lord to recalibrate and detox my heart was because of something buried within that made me susceptible to deception and led me outside of His will. Remember Scripture calls the heart deceitful (Jeremiah 17:9) and says only God knows the heart (1 Kings 8:39). You cannot know or understand what's in your heart without help from God.

I'm sure you've heard popular advice on television to "follow your heart" or the saying that "the heart doesn't lie." But Jesus said evil thoughts, adultery, sexual immorality, slander, and lies comes from desires within our heart (Matthew 15:19). Because of how I felt about Isaac, I desperately wanted to follow my heart, but my heart was filled with lies.

119

Have you ever believed something to be good with your whole heart, but later discovered it wasn't? John Bevere, in his book *Good or God*, provides an excellent illustration of how Eve believed it was okay to eat the fruit from the tree of the knowledge of good and evil because it *looked* good but later realized she and Adam were deceived by a lie wrapped in truth from Satan (Genesis 3:1-7). Bevere points out that Eve was deceived by evil masked as good. He argues that there are things in this world that seem good to us but are evil in God's eyes.

Everything about my relationship with Isaac seemed good, but because he wasn't divorced, our relationship was a sin in God's eyes (Proverbs 14:12). There are things in our hearts and minds that masquerade as the truth but are actually lies and evil in God's eyes. Recalibration, the examination and repositioning of the heart by God, is needed to expose faults (Psalm 19:12-13), and reveal His truth.

Release Detox

Let's just acknowledge releasing someone you love, who occupies your whole heart, is incredibly difficult, particularly when you hope the relationship is temporarily on hold. I held hope in my heart because I believed Isaac was the one. Let me remind you of the prophetic word I received; the man God had for me was tall, would fly in, look for me to be his future wife, and have a ministry, and would partner with me in my purpose. Isaac was over six feet tall and had a ministry of helping young boys, and he flew into the event. Just for the record, I didn't think every tall man I encountered was the one God spoke of in the prophecy. But in Isaac's case, I did.

I had a conversation with God that went something like this. "Lord, you said the man You had for me would fly in." The Lord replied, "He did fly in." When the Lord reminded me that Isaac flew in to the event, I thought He was bringing me confirmation that Isaac was the one. Keep in mind that, after we ended the relationship, Isaac

120

came looking for me. More specifically, when I saw Isaac at the event, he said, "I'm so happy to see you. I came here looking for you." While this may sound like a stretch, that's what I believed. This alone made me reluctant to release him and caused me to have hope that one day, we'd be together as husband and wife.

One of the most dangerous mistakes I could have made was not releasing Isaac back to God. I heard a powerful sermon by Touré Roberts, who told his congregation it's more important to awaken to your purpose *before* you get married. If you marry someone before you know your purpose, the relationship may struggle because your callings and purposes may not be equally yoked. And at the time, I did not know my purpose.

Despite my reluctance, I released Isaac in my heart. There were three reasons I was able to successfully detox. First, I had complete confidence that the Lord would deliver me from the pain of losing Isaac as He did after my marriage ended. Second, because I was able to release my children, my most precious gifts from God, and trust Him, I knew I could do the same with someone I thought was the one. Third, I firmly believed in my heart a saying I've heard Pastor Howard-John Wesley of Alfred Street Baptist Church say, "God *always* has another!"

Signs you may need a detox include the following:
- ∂ Feeling rejected
- ∂ Self-doubt and issues with self-worth
- ∂ Self-sabotaging behaviors
- ∂ Feeling depressed, worried, anxious, and/or depressed
- ∂ Reliving and replaying the pain
- ∂ Feeling guilty, angry, unforgiving, and/or bitter

As you walk through any of the detox processes with God, ponder the following questions:
1. Why do I want to date?

2. Am I ready to date?
3. Are my reasons for wanting to date selfishly motivated?
4. Do I pray without ceasing or run away from God when I knowingly, carelessly, or unintentionally make mistakes in dating?
5. What type(s) of detox(es) do I need? Emotional, psychological, physical, or romantic?
6. Do I trust that God has someone for me?

Once you've answered these questions, pray and ask God to search your heart, create in you a new heart, and restore your joy. Here are a few scriptures to pray over yourself during your detox:

"Search me, God, and know my heart; test me and know my anxious thoughts" (Psalm 139:23).

"Create in me a pure heart, O God, and renew a steadfast spirit within me. Do not cast me from your presence or take your Holy Spirit from me. Restore to me the joy of your salvation and grant me a willing spirit, to sustain me" (Psalm 51:10-12).

Help me to follow Jesus and be more attentive to His voice (John 10:27) and not pursue all the ungodly desires that spring from my heart.

CHAPTER 9
Season of Awakening

Be strong and take heart, all you who hope for the LORD!
(Psalm 31:24)

WAITING ON GOD

Four years after I moved out and my divorce was final, the roller coaster called my life started to stabilize. I finally received a raise and bonus at work, and my finances were manageable. I was awarded child support and alimony. I started a doctorate program, and I was finally emotionally sober. I found rest in my spirit and peace of mind that had been absent in previous years. Because I experienced so much turbulence from the divorce, I was thankful for stability and normalcy. However, I wanted more out of life.

I wanted to buy a home closer to my office because the one-hour commute each way was exhausting. I also wanted a home with a large backyard, where my children had the freedom to make as much noise as they wanted. It was hard to contain the energy and rambunctiousness of two children with apartment-style living. I needed to make a change in my living situation.

The place where we lived was beautiful, but the rent increased by more than 10% with every lease renewal. When I first moved in, the rent was $1,700 a month, but by year five, the rent was $3,100. An alternative option was for me to rent a home closer to where I worked and my kids attended school. I went online and found a few home rentals, but most of the homes near my office, located in safe and desirable neighborhoods, were unaffordable. I looked at a small three-bedroom home in the Oakland Hills but the move-in cost was $10,000, typical for the Bay Area.

While there were so many benefits to renting an apartment as a single mother, given the hike in rent, it seemed practical to purchase instead. I prayed and asked God for a new home and to bring me favor as I moved forward. Initially, I was apprehensive about taking on the responsibility that comes along with a new home, such as maintenance, insurance, and property taxes. I was also scared because I'd gone through the humiliation of a short sale for a home. But I believed homeownership was the best solution.

To educate myself, I attended a homebuyers' workshop. I also reached out to a friend who was a real estate agent and who connected me to a broker. I discovered I was eligible to participate in a first-time homebuyer program because more than three years had passed since I short sold my home. I prequalified for $575,000, which was low in the San Francisco Bay Area. At the time, the housing market was ridiculously high. For a 2,000-square-foot home, depending on the location, the average cost was between $575,000 and $650,000.

Based on my prequalified amount, I couldn't buy the type of single-family, modern home desired in an area that would save on my commute, which was discouraging. Each time I stepped forward in faith, I ran into one roadblock after the next. For instance, the agent I worked with seemed unengaged when I asked about viewing specific properties, and she misplaced my paperwork twice. I was frustrated. I called my mother to tell her about the roadblocks I encountered, and she said, "Maybe God is telling you no." At that moment, I knew that she was right. I told her, "That's all I needed to hear." I immediately told the agent and broker I'd decided to wait to buy a home and stopped pursuing homeownership.

Stepping Out in Faith

God never told me to pursue purchasing a home. I prayed He would bless me as I moved forward with something I had in mind for myself, but not something that was God-led. Although God put the desire for a home in my heart, I was guilty of stepping ahead of His plan for my life. I thought because I believed and prayed for God's covering for a new home that it was okay to move forward. In retrospect, I wanted Him to follow *my* plan. But how many times have you believed God had greater and started moving in a certain direction only to discover God never said yes?

At the time, I called what I did stepping out in faith. But what does that mean? Does it mean acting in the absence of God's no and trusting and believing He will prevent you from moving forward if you're outside of His will? The Bible describes faith as the substance of things hoped for and the evidence of things not seen (Hebrews 11:1).

I'm sure there are different thoughts and interpretations of what stepping out in faith looks like and what people believe. Here's what I think, stepping out in faith is when God has *called* you to do something, and even though you don't have all the information and you're uncertain or frightened, you move forward in faith, trusting Him.

Consider how Abraham stepped out in faith when God told him to leave his homeland, or how Moses moved forward in faith when God told him to go to Egypt.

In my case, I stepped out based on my own plan and called it faith because I prayed and believed God would grant my prayer request or intervene. The challenge, sometimes, with waiting on God is that His yes or no isn't always immediate. And when that happens, the temptation is to move forward anyway.

Closed Doors

I also thought if I headed in the wrong direction or strayed from His will, He would inevitably redirect me. Is it incorrect to assume God will close doors if I travel down the wrong path? I was recently reminded of when Abimelech king of Gerar, believing Sarah was Abraham's sister and not his wife, took her. The Lord intervened and prevented Abimelech from touching her (Genesis 20:6). There are numerous examples in scripture and in our everyday lives when God intervened as well as times when He did not interfere with choices made by His people. Did the Lord interfere when Sarah decided, and Abraham agreed, to have Sarah's maidservant Hagar bear the child promised to them by God? No. Did God stop David when he decided to sleep with Bathsheba and have her husband killed? No. There are times when God intervenes on our behalf and others when He does not.

While I was at peace with the decision not to pursue becoming a homebuyer, I felt stuck in my situation. I needed His direction. I wondered, *"God why do I need to wait to buy a house? Lord, when will you open a door for me?"* The truth was God knew I still had more than $350,000 of debt remaining, and it wasn't the right time for me to purchase. It would have been so easy for me to get upset and distracted by God's no. But I discovered it was easier for me to trust God rather than fall into depression and despair when I didn't receive something I sought through prayer. Based on my experience with God over the years, and the many times He delivered me from calamity and bad decisions, I knew He would never withhold anything from me that was for my good. Therefore, I waited and prayed.

How You Wait

Waiting on God can be challenging but necessary in the life of a believer. Waiting gives you opportunities to grow in wisdom and bear godly fruit. But at times, it can feel like a punishment rather than waiting for God to give birth to a blessing. Waiting can cause you to become discouraged, anxious, worried, and it can create a crisis that rages within and leads you to question and doubt God. Although God knows what you want and need before you ask (Matthews 6:8), waiting on Him to fulfill His promises can be excruciating, depending on how you choose to wait.

Joyce Meyer, one of my favorite female teachers of the Word, tells believers we can choose to wait on God impatiently or with an expectant attitude. Consider the impatience of Sarah in waiting on the Lord for twenty-five years to fulfill His promise of a son through whom the covenant would be fulfilled. Her impatience gave birth to Ishmael, who the Lord described as a wild donkey of a man who lived in hostility with his brothers (Genesis 16:12). On the other hand, we can wait expectantly, knowing He is working on our behalf. David waited expectantly, for over twenty years, to become king of Israel, and Joseph waited for his dream of leading others to come to pass. Even Jesus waited for about eighteen years before He started His ministry. And during that time, He "grew in wisdom and stature, and in favor with God and man" (Luke 2:52). Growth in character occurs when you wait on God, but there may also be a delay in growth if you wait angrily or impatiently instead of expectantly.

I was in a season of waiting on God not just for a house, but also for a new job opportunity with more compensation. After working for the same company for ten years, I was ready for a change. I outgrew the role. I believed there was nothing else that I could add and my passion for the work disappeared. I was bored. I'd also worked in my field for so long that I wanted to advance to another level. If I'm being honest, I grew tired of watching most of my friends climb the career ladder and seemingly soar, while I stayed in the same place, in the same role.

A part of me felt like I was missing out on something. I saw friends with lofty job titles and the financial means to travel to extravagant places and partake in what many people would consider the finer things in life. I compared where I was with where they were, not out of jealousy or envy but out of lack and impatience. I too wanted a lofty job title, financial means, and to join my friends in accessing opportunities. But in order to have that, I believed I needed to leave my job because something better was on the other side of feeling unfilled.

In addition to experiencing boredom and lack of fulfillment, I was frustrated. Over a ten-year period, I had a total of ten bosses. Some I enjoyed, and others worked my nerves. God placed me under each person for specific reasons. I remember thinking He was teaching me about humility, submitting to authority, and learning to operate in obedience. On occasion, I suffered from pride and haughtiness. I had a know-it-all attitude.

When I reached a point when I believed I couldn't take it any longer, I prayed and asked God, "Is my season up at this job? When will you open a door for another job?" But each time, I heard the Holy Spirit say, *"My grace is sufficient."* God was calling me to remain in my current situation (1 Corinthians 7:20), but that's not what I wanted at the time. I was ready to promote and soar.

Then the Lord brought to my mind a word I received from a friend who told me God would use me to minister to other people. She told me God would elevate me to speak to others about overcoming brokenness and use my testimony to heal people. First, I wondered, "Why would God want to use me?" I was afraid to pray out loud, couldn't recite or remember Bible verses, didn't have a recognizable gift or talent, and had made too many mistakes in my life. Second, I wondered, "What does me not being able to buy a house or get another job have to do with God wanting to use me?" I didn't give it much thought beyond the questions I pondered. I wasn't exactly sure why

God chose that moment to remind me of something a friend told me several years earlier.

When it became clear God wasn't releasing me from my position, rather than get upset, anxious, or impatient, as I did in the past, I was thankful, knowing He was working on my behalf. Jesus reminds us both He and God are working day and night on our behalf (John 5:17). He does not sleep or slumber (Psalm 121:4). He bears my burdens daily (Psalm 68:19). There's something peaceful in knowing God is working for me. Instead of worrying about when my waiting season would be over, I became thankful, knowing the Holy Spirit was alongside me, waiting, guiding, and leading.

UNQUALIFIED

Once I thanked God for His goodness and decided to wait patiently on His promises, my prayer life began to change. Rather than constantly pray about my situation, I started asking Him to *use me* to bless others. More specifically, I asked Him to send me those who needed encouragement and upliftment. This was the kingdom work God needed from me while I waited to walk in my purpose. Although I was ill-equipped and, frankly, unqualified to minister to others, God used my willing spirit to help those in need—whether I could quote scriptures or not. He also used my natural abilities (encourager, listener, worth builder) and my professional background of counseling others in combination with my desire to please Him (Philippians 2:13).

God honored my prayer and sent men and women from different ethnic and cultural backgrounds, believers and nonbelievers, married, divorced, and single people. I spoke about His goodness and the ways He delivered me from turmoil. As I shared my testimony, the Holy Spirit brought forth scriptures and sermons I previously read and heard to offer godly advice to people at my office. It was the most shocking experience. I was amazed at how God used me. Word must have spread in my office because several colleagues asked me to pray for them in the areas of finances, relationships, advancement, anger, regret, theft, frustration, and the list goes on. Although I was apprehensive about praying out loud, I let God use my mouth.

God was moving in such a mighty way in my job! The same job I wanted to leave. It never occurred to me, when I started praying and asking God to heal me from past wounds, that He wanted to use me to bring words of healing to others. He used me to intercede, introduce, and invite others into a deeper relationship with Him. I witnessed Him open doors and bless my colleagues' prayer requests, such as job advancement, new homes, and restored relationships.

Although I was genuinely happy for each person whose petition the Lord granted, I asked God, "When will I be next?" Perhaps He heard my heart say, "What about me?" Over the next year, I openly prayed and ministered to others at my office, all while my boss devalued my work, overlooked my potential, treated me differently from other members of the team, and made it a point to monitor my comings and goings. Added to this, I saw an interoffice email in which a colleague spoke negatively about me to the senior leadership team, accusing me of wrongdoing. The next time I saw him, he smiled, hugged me, and kissed me on the cheek. That was my first Judas-like experience.

It seemed like the more I prayed and tried to serve the needs of my colleagues, the more attacks I underwent from the enemy. There were days when it seemed like it was one blow or attack after the next. The enemy wanted me to quit ministering and focus on the way I was being treated by my boss to distract me from what God wanted. Although difficult, I pressed in harder and continued to labor for Christ.

Life Lesson #17
Let God use you for His glory while you wait.

GOD'S PROMOTION

In an unexpected way, God answered my prayer for Him to open a door to opportunity. He promoted me to another level in my faith instead of promoting me into another position. I wanted to leave prematurely, and He needed me to stay. He wanted to use me to be a blessing to others instead of asking Him to always bless me. I wanted to do something great in my life, but God didn't want greatness, He wanted me to reach a state where I was usable. But before God could use me, he had to prepare me for my divine purpose.

> *Key Thought*
> *Waiting is a blessing from God. He loves you and wants you to be the person He intended you to be. He knows spiritual growth requires time and patience.*

Preparation for my calling

When I asked Him to send me people who needed encouragement, one of my natural gifts, I unknowingly stepped into my calling. Calling is the road we travel in life, once we accept the invitation from Christ, to reach our purpose. Calling is connected to your relationship with God. Without a personal relationship with Him, you won't learn what He has called you to do. You may know you have certain gifts, talents, and abilities, but you won't have the spiritual awareness that comes from using those gifts for God's kingdom.

God used the pain from my divorce to give birth to my calling of ministering to single, married, and divorced believers who, at some point in life, lost hope or who have been overlooked, broken, and discarded by someone they once loved. Remember the prophetic word that God would use me to minister to others? Well, He used me to share my testimony of deliverance, comfort those who experienced similar challenges, and reveal how He helped me overcome my seasons of struggle.

There were so many people in my office who did not know Christ and His redeeming love and others who were raised to believe in Him but did not have a relationship with Him. They were lost. Think about how Jesus described the crowd He ministered to as harassed, helpless, and thirsty souls, like sheep without a shepherd. He told the disciples the harvest was plentiful, but the laborers were few (Matthew 9:35-37). Perhaps Jesus was metaphorically referring to their spiritual state of being lost and pointing out that there were few laborers to lead them to Christ. Whatever the case, I believe He was calling me to be a laborer, to serve, and to point people to Him, but He knew I was unprepared. While I ministered to people at work and to friends, God revealed there were bad habits and areas of my life that needed to be cleansed.

1. My Unclean Mouth

One of my biggest challenges that needed attention was my excessive use of profanity. I grew up around people who used three, four, five, and six-letter words to express irritation and anger, and at times, just because. And like a virus, as I was exposed to the profanity, it eventually spread to me. There were times when my words were vulgar, harsh, or mean-spirited, not always purposefully but because I was unaware of how my words affected people. In my youth, my tongue was explosive and sharp as a sword.

As I grew older, my words weren't as vulgar and mean-, but they still had the potential to ruin my calling. The Bible says the tongue is restless, filled with evil, poisonous (James 3:8), and cannot be tamed unless God intervenes (Ephesians 4:22-24). Further, it states we use our tongue to bless God and curse others (James 3:9-10). Can you imagine me trying to tell others about Jesus and using vulgar, slanderous, and hurtful language that would cause people to reject Christ?

Back then, my best friend told me God could still use me even though my mouth was unsaved. It's true God can use someone with an unclean mouth because He does not require us to be perfect. But in looking at the life of Jesus, who is the standard for Christian living, you see He didn't curse even when he was angry or mistreated.

I can't quite pinpoint when my desire to stop using profanity changed, but it did. It didn't happen overnight, but there was something different about the way I spoke. As I spent more time in His presence, I felt Him calling me to live higher and put aside unwholesome and filthy language (Colossians 3:8), and to use my words to edify Him.

2. Bad Company

Another challenge was that the friends I spent time with regularly used vulgar and obscene language. When I was around certain friends, my tongue was unbridled. As I reflect on some of the crude words I've used in the past, particularly when I decided to hang out with certain people, I cringe. It's not because I think that I was better than anyone then or even now, but because there's a bigger part of me that doesn't want to grieve the Holy Spirit with my language (Ephesians 4:30-32).

Do you have friends who are incredibly funny and frequently express themselves using obscenities? Like the ones who have you doubled over, teary eyed, and screaming laughing, all while trying not to pee on yourself? Do you have friends who remind you of your favorite comedian? Well, those are the friends I have. Like me, they grew up around family and friends who frequently used the language you hear on Hip-Hop XL satellite radio. Like me, they were raised on music from 2Pac, Notorious BIG, Snoop, and Ice Cube and movies like *Menace to Society*, *Dead Presidents*, and *Boys in the Hood*.

133

Now, is there something inherently wrong with associating with friends who curse? Not necessarily, but I do recommend you pray about anyone y0u choose to spend time with. Some people can help propel you forward in your calling and purpose and others can detract from it. I know how easy it is to be influenced by others. The longer you expose yourself to people, the more you start to sound alike. Over time, I found myself mimicking their words, habits, and behaviors, while others mimicked my tone and words.

As funny and vulgar as some of my friends were, I chose to distance myself (not unfriend) from people who triggered my *desire* to use unclean language. Believers are warned that bad friends corrupt good character (1 Corinthians 15:33). Before you judge me, I think that it's important to know thyself. When I'm around certain people, the temptation to curse is powerful. Choosing to create distance wasn't about being "holier than thou," but I couldn't follow Jesus wholeheartedly and repeatedly give in to my temptations. The Bible states, "Those who consider themselves religious and yet do not keep a tight rein on their tongues deceive themselves, and their religion is worthless" (James 1:26). I couldn't be a walking contradiction, saying I love the Lord and at the same time loving culture. I couldn't serve two masters (1 John 2:15). My words and actions either show I love God and hate the world or love the world and hate God.

3. Soft and Meek

Ministering to others requires a certain amount of sensitivity and meekness. There was hardness in me that developed during my younger years. Therefore, there were things the Lord needed to put in and bring forth to help soften my words and demeanor, such as humility, kindness, and patience. He also needed to soften my tough exterior, so I could lovingly invite others to explore a relationship with Him.

God supernaturally softened my toughness and replaced it with tenderheartedness, gentleness, and humble mindedness. You might wonder how I knew God softened me. It was the strangest thing, but when I told people about the goodness of God and how He saved me, I wept. For someone who didn't cry much, it was alarming. In the past, I'd cried over painful experiences, but not much outside of that. At times, I felt emotionally void and unsure why there was so much emptiness inside me. But after my encounter with Christ, it didn't take much to make me cry. All the unhealthy emotions I kept bottled up inside and years of toughness unexpectedly poured out. Even now as I type these words, my eyes have started to water.

I felt overwhelmed by how God changed me from the inside out. The toughness I clung tightly to in my youth and young adult years melted away. With the softness came an abundance of empathy, compassion, and gentleness. So many times, I sobbed when I spoke of God's mercifulness and unyielding love. My kids often wondered why I cried so much, and I told them they were tears of joy. If someone near me or over the phone started to cry, tears freely fell from my eyes. In church, when the congregation praised and worshiped, out of nowhere, I cried like a baby. I barely recognized myself. I experienced was a spiritual cleansing. It was a rebirth, and I became a new creature in Christ, as the old, tough me passed away (2 Corinthians 5:17).

Once my toughness softened, I became meek; the Holy Spirit taught me how to exercise patience and spiritual restraint. Meekness is simply power under control. It's a virtue drawn from God. What that looked like for me was remaining quiet when someone attempted to be disrespectful or walking away from conflict, knowing I could have "clapped back" with harsh words or taken more drastic actions. Instead, the Holy Spirit taught me remaining quiet and walking away from conflict weren't signs of weakness, but signs of strength and humility.

Consider for a moment this idea of meekness representing strength. David, the man who defeated Goliath and many of his adversaries, was the same man who ran from King Saul. He didn't run because he was fearful Saul could defeat him. He showed strength when he ran away, knowing he could have killed Saul when the opportunity was presented. When the Pharisees criticized, slandered, and plotted to kill Jesus, He denounced the hypocrisy of the Jewish leaders, but Jesus didn't clap back. He didn't retaliate, threaten, or call a legion of angels from heaven to smite those who offended Him (1 Peter 2:23). Instead, He demonstrated meekness by submitting His will to God and giving Himself as a living sacrifice.

4. Not Listening

The fourth area that required God's attention was my struggle with listening attentively. Listening to someone takes effort and requires concentration, focus, and awareness of what is being said, whereas hearing doesn't require focus or awareness. My mind and ears were undisciplined. Scripture says we should be quick to listen, slow to speak, and slow to anger (James 1:19). Well, I was quick to speak and slow to listen.

The Lord revealed I had several bad listening habits that would interfere with my calling if not corrected. First, He revealed I tended to rush someone to finish what they needed to say and cut them off if they took too long to get to the point. I assumed I knew what they wanted to say before they finished speaking. I tried to finish what I believed they wanted to say and compose an answer before they finished speaking. I was an impatient listener. Scripture points out that "Fools find no pleasure in understanding but delight in airing their own opinions" (Proverbs 18:2) and "to answer before listening, that is folly and shame" (Proverbs 18:13). My failure to listen was a stumbling block to ministry.

136

I listen to people constantly as a part of my job, where I need to remain focused. However, outside of work, I find it hard and mentally taxing to listen to someone who has difficulty getting to the point. I've discovered people rarely start with the salient points, so I tend to check out of the conversation or try to rush the speaker to get to the point. Don't judge me. God is still working with me on this. I'm progressing, but not perfect.

5. Easily Distracted and Unfocused

The Lord also revealed I was easily distracted and unfocused in my interactions with people. Over the years, I told myself I was a skilled at multitasking. There were times when someone walked into my office to say something to me, and I listened to music, composed an email, and searched for something else on my split monitor, all while I told the person, "I'm listening." But the reality was I only partially heard what they said because I was distracted.

Interestingly, I was unaware of how easily distracted and unfocused I was in conversations until God pointed it out to me. In fact, it was the Holy Spirit who quickened my spirit and told me I needed to be more focused when people spoke to me. He told me when someone walked into my office I needed to stop typing, turn the music off, turn my chair around to face them, and give them eye contact. He also told me not to turn around and look at my computer screen or check my cell phone when I received a notification. This was especially hard because my mind was conditioned to respond to new email alerts because I didn't like it when my inbox was full. I didn't want to miss important text messages in case they concerned my children. Truth be told, giving someone my full attention was challenging. I was accustomed to distraction. Let's be honest. How many of us are guilty of multitasking, half listening, and allowing distractions to interfere with active listening?

I even had the bad habit of scrolling on Facebook or Instagram, watching video clips, or playing a game on my cell phone while someone was speaking to me. One day, I went out to lunch at The Cheesecake Factory with my best friend. As soon as the waitress escorted us to our table and the waiter brought our beverages, I reached in my purse and pulled out my cell phone to play one of my many games. "Are you seriously playing your game while I'm talking to you?" she asked me. I replied, "Yes, but I'm listening to what you're saying."

My friend challenged me and told me I was not listening to her. The only reason I put my cell phone away and stopped playing Words with Friends was because she would have nagged me through the entire lunch. I was annoyed that she wanted all my attention. I'm pretty sure she'll roll her eyes as she reads this, but the truth was I was preoccupied with what I wanted to do instead of enjoying the conversation.

I'm certain I've missed many key points people have tried to convey to me throughout the years, all because I was distracted and unfocused. I'm sure I'm not the only person who struggles in this area. Recently, I literally on the phone with a friend, to whom I hadn't spoken in years, and I had to consciously not turn on my television or open apps or social media while she was speaking. This is one area where I die daily. It's still not natural for me to stop, drop everything I'm doing, and give someone my full attention, but when the Holy Spirit prompts me, I immediately become aware and correct my behavior.

6. Too Busy

In addition to being an impatient listener who was easily distracted, another bad habit that I struggled with was feeling irritated and annoyed if someone interrupted me while I was busy. After God allowed me to start my workplace ministry, someone walked into my office wanting advice on a personal matter. I turned off my music, took my hands off the keyboard, and turned around to give them my undivided attention. However, I felt irritated that they interrupted me because I had a deadline to meet.

I'm certain that the person wasn't aware of how I felt on the inside, but God knew. Remember I was the one who asked the Lord to send me people who needed encouraging. Ministry and being used by God isn't always convenient. I wanted the people He sent to come when it was convenient for me and not when I had a work deadline or when I was trying to rush off to a meeting or leave to pick my kids up from school.

In those situations, I said a quick prayer and asked God to help me release the feeling of irritation and to restore my time, so I wouldn't miss an important deadline, meeting, or the chance to avoid the traffic jam on the freeway after I picked up my kids. And each time I blessed those in need, I no longer felt irritated, whether I was able to get to where I was going on time or not. Simply put, I let it go.

Life Lesson #18
Ask God to show you things and bad habits that interfere with your calling.

After the Holy Spirit alerted me to my behaviors over several days, or perhaps weeks, I asked Him to help me give my mind over to what He called me to do and to focus. In looking at the life of Jesus, I see the perfect example of how to behave when challenged with listening, friendships, gentleness, discipline, and patience. He always listened attentively as a way to demonstrate care and love. He was patient, gentle, and kind with those He encountered. He was not angry, irritated, or annoyed when He was interrupted. He wasn't distracted by busyness, people, or things. He stayed focused on what the Father called Him to do (Luke 2:49), all of which He was able to do because of His obedient nature and relationship with the Father.

Looking back, I was consumed with wanting to leave my company for a higher-paying position to experience abundance, keep up with the successes of others, and avoid dealing with a difficult boss, all of which were self-absorbed reasons. However, God used my job as my mission field. He was preparing me there, but it wasn't my life's mission.

At the time, God didn't want to send me to another company or city to share my testimony and minister to others. He used me exactly where He placed me. And although the circumstances at my job were not ideal, God gave me a chance to help and comfort others where I worked while my character was developing.

> *Key Thought:*
> *What if your unanswered prayer isn't God withholding your blessing, but God helping you grow and mature to handle the blessing He has for you?*

PURPOSE UNFOLDING

During my season of waiting, I became aware that God was leading me towards my divine purpose. Touré Roberts, in his book *Awakening Purpose* argues that, because God created us with His purpose in mind, we do not discover our purpose, rather we are awakened to it. He describes the awakening as the awareness of purpose, something that was lost in translation when we were born, to a state of knowing why you are here and what you are supposed to do. Marshawn Evans Daniels, in her book *Believe Bigger: Discover the Path to Your Life Purpose*, adds to this idea by suggesting purpose is always with us, even when we are unaware, and will be revealed over time. This is a great depiction of what happened to me. Before my ex-husband chose to leave our marriage, I was unaware that God created me with His purpose in mind. But as I've traveled through each season after my divorce, I've become cognizant that God created me for something specific and beyond my imagination.

While I have an awareness that God created me for His purpose (Romans 8:28), my purpose, which includes writing this book to share my story, is continually unfolding. As I traveled down the road of my calling, I ran headlong into my purpose, but I don't think there's a straight line to purpose. I don't believe one day you wake up and your purpose is revealed. Awakening to purpose gradually happens as you zigzag through different seasons in life and as your spirit matures and character develops. It's a progressive process in which your faith is tested, stretched, and strengthened. Your purpose continues to unfold as you fix your mind on God, surrender to His will, and allow Him to transform your heart, habits, mindsets, and behaviors. As you evolve, die to self, and obey His word, the old you passes away, the new you emerges, and you advance towards or in purpose.

During my season of waiting, I saw how God was strategically positioning me in the right places (whether they were places that I wanted to be or not), at the appointed time, and with preordained people (those who opposed and supported me). But while I waited to *become* the person He created me to be and enter into the fullness of my unique purpose, I glorified His name.

Glorifying God

Everyone on this planet was created to glorify God (Isaiah 43:7). Rick Warren in his book, *The Purpose Driven Life*, argued that our purpose in life is greater than our personal comfort and the pursuit of happiness. Rather, a purpose-driven life, he argued, should be modeled after Jesus, which brings glory to God. He further suggested that God is calling us to do the same. The Bible says, "In the same way, let your light shine before others, that they may see your good deeds and glorify your Father in heaven" (Matthew 5:16). Each time that I chose to behave like Jesus, meaning extend kindness and compassion, give generously without expecting anything in return, obey God, forgive those who hurt me, and offered love, I let my light shine before others and glorified Him. When I shared my testimony of how God delivered me from betrayal, rejection, and broken trust, I brought God glory. I told people about His redemptive power, merciful spirit, understanding heart, majesty, splendor, and never-ending love, which further glorified Him.

Comforting Others

Bringing words of encouragement and comfort to those in need, helped me grow closer to who Christ intended me to be, which further brought Him glory. Consider Paul's words.

Praise be to the God and Father of our LORD Jesus Christ, the Father of compassion and the God of all comfort, who comforts us in all our troubles, so that we can comfort those in any trouble with the comfort we ourselves receive from God.
(2 Corinthians 1:3-4)

Because of God's mercy and grace, not only was I now able to comfort people I knew at work and close friends, I did so with strangers as well. Think about how effortless it is to comfort people who we know. When crisis and chaos is at their front door, it's easier to offer whatever comfort and support is needed. But weigh Luke's words (Luke 6:32-36).

If you love those who love you, what credit is that to you?
Even sinners love those who love them.

142

And if you do good to those who are good to you,
what credit is that to you? Even sinners do that.
And if you lend to those from whom you expect repayment,
what credit is that to you? Even sinners lend to sinners,
expecting to be repaid in full.
But love your enemies, do good to them,
and lend to them without expecting to get anything back.
Then your reward will be great, and you will be
children of the Most High, because he is kind to the ungrateful and
wicked.
Be merciful, just as your Father is merciful.

The truth was, before my divorce, I only comforted people who I knew and not people I met at work or otherwise. But after my divorce and when God softened me, I became more sensitive and readily prayed for strangers who I encountered as well as people who I knew disliked me.

I remember when the Lord called me to pray for someone who I worked with and I knew that this person absolutely DID NOT LIKE ME. No matter how nice I was or the many times that I offered the hand of fellowship, she still spoke negatively about me to my colleagues all while smiling in my face. Well, the Lord told me to go to this person and pray with her because she had been rejected and was sad. It was the last thing that I wanted to do. In fact, I told the Lord that I did not want to pray for or with her. I remember feeling put off by God, but out of obedience I did it. The truth is, although I humbly went to her and watched her weep, and she said that she was thankful that God sent me, it did not change how she treated me. She was still unkind, deceptive, and abusive towards others. But perhaps God was testing me to see if I would comfort and show love to those who opposed and seemingly hated me the way Christ offered love to those who opposed Him.

I also remember when I was on a cruise with a friend and there were people sitting at the bar who expressed deep pain over things happening in their lives. These people were complete strangers. Rather than walk away or ignore their words, I engaged in conversations, offered words of encouragement and comfort, and prayed for or with them. My friend found it odd that so many people naturally gravitated towards me and shared their problems. She even expressed slight irritation that so many people approached me. But I knew that God wanted me to listen, offer comfort, show compassion, and pray on their behalf. Besides, I also knew that those people were not attracted to me because I had something that someone else did not, but they were drawn to my spirit and the light of God present in me.

It's Not About Me

I've come to the realization that sharing my testimony, encouraging others, and offering comfort to those who have been afflicted was not entirely about who I was or was becoming, but about *who* God is. One of my favorite pastors, Dr. Dharius Daniels, who I watch on YouTube, illustrated a similar thought when he told the well-known story of how Shadrach, Meshach, and Abednego were thrown into the fiery furnace for refusing to bow down and worship King Nebuchadnezzar's golden image (Daniel 3). When the three Hebrews boys didn't burn alive and there was no evidence of their hair being singed, King Nebuchadnezzar said, "Praise be to the God of Shadrach, Meshach and Abednego, who has sent his angel and rescued his servants! They trusted in him and defied the king's command and were willing to give up their lives rather than serve or worship any god except their own God. Therefore I decree that the people of any nation or language who say anything against the God of Shadrach, Meshach and Abednego be cut into pieces and their houses be turned into piles of rubble, for no other god can save in this way." (Daniel 3:28-29).

144

The pastor emphasized the point that God may have delivered the three Hebrew boys from the furnace so a powerful king and his people would come to *know* the God of Shadrach, Meshach, and Abednego. In other words, God's blessings and our trials are not always about you or me. Sometimes, they're a means for others to meet and know Him *through* you and me. Even Jesus dedicated His time on earth to make the name of the Father known and to glorify Him (John 17:26), and He commissioned believers to do the same.

CATAPULTING

Ministering to the needs of others did not change my desire to leave my job. I simply became content where I was during that season. I continued to pray for a breakthrough, a sign from the Lord that it was time to move forward. A year later, I heard a preacher and teacher of the Word say, "Maybe you're not waiting on God, but maybe God is waiting on you." Taking that message to heart, I started my search for a new position. I thought, *Surely, God wants me to start looking for a job.* For some reason, I was waiting for God to literally drop a job opportunity into my lap until I heard that message. And again, I asked for God's favor. This time I prayed that God open doors only He could open and close doors that needed to be closed. Like Moses, I did not want to walk into any situation without God's presence (Exodus 33:15). Despite my prayers, I didn't hear a yes or no from God. My thought was that if God's hand wasn't in it, then He would close those doors.

I saw several positions that matched my skill set and interest and offered compensation within the range I wanted. After three grueling interviews without a job offer, I decided to wait until God opened a door. A few weeks went by, and a friend from work brought me a job description for a position in southern California that mirrored my role and paid $20,000 more than my current salary. I looked over the qualifications and noticed I had all the requirements. The position seemed to be tailored-made for me. The only problem was that the position was located one hour outside of Los Angeles. On the plus side, it was in the exact city where my parents resided. While I didn't have a desire to move back to southern California, I had a knowing in my spirit that God was presenting me with an opportunity.

I was scared because I didn't want to move my kids away from their father, and I wasn't ready to give up the life I'd built. I had finally found a church home for my children and me that I loved. Why would God want me to apply for a position in southern California when He knew my desire to remain in the Bay Area? Although I never specified a location, my prayer and preference were for a higher paying position in northern California, but God had other plans.

I tried to talk myself out of applying. I reasoned within myself that He never told me to apply nor did He say I would get the job if I applied. Like Gideon, I wanted confirmation (Judges 6:39) that the job opportunity was from Him. Not all open doors are from God, but I had a knowing within that it was God who used my co-worker to present me with this opportunity.

I waited to hear from God before I applied. One weekend, my best friend's mother was in town, and she gave me a word from the Lord that He was going to move me from northern California. She didn't know about my request to the Lord or that I was searching for another job. But it was the confirmation I needed.

Two years before God presented this opportunity, I talked with a close friend about my financial struggles and single motherhood challenges, and I shared that there were no new opportunities within my organization on the horizon. She suggested I move back to southern California to be near my parents, so they could help me with my kids, but I was vehement in my decision to remain in northern California. I dismissed her suggestion. I simply could not see myself starting over again.

Even after I received confirmation, I didn't immediately apply for the position. I hesitated. It's amazing how we pray and ask God for opportunities and when those opportunities are presented, we can't see what God is showing us, so we talk ourselves out of what He has for us. I actually received a knowing in my spirit from the Lord and a confirmation through a friend, but the next step was mine to take. God presents us with opportunities daily, but we can easily pass up those opportunities when they don't align with what we think or feel. *I* wanted to stay in the Bay Area. *I* didn't want relocated. *I* wanted God to give me the desires of my heart, which was to remain in a specific city with a different job prospect. Finally, rather than succumb to fear and stubbornness, I stepped out in faith and applied for the position.

Four months after I applied for the job, I received an email for an interview. I purchased a plane ticket, flew to southern California, and interviewed with a panel. Afterwards, my father asked me how I did, and I cried. He told me I probably did well. I told him, "I'm not crying because I was horrible. I'm crying because I think they're going to offer me the job." If they offered me the position, I would need to pack up my life and move. The day after I interviewed, I received a call from the human resources department to return for a second interview, and two days later I was offered the job.

CHAPTER 10
Season of Forgiveness

*Let us not become weary in doing good, for in at the proper time we
will reap a harvest if we do not give up.*
(Galatians 6:9)

EXPECT THE UNEXPECTED

*C*an you to start within the next three weeks? Those were the
words from my new employer. Everything happened so
quickly. I wanted the pace to slow down. I hadn't planned to
start my new job that soon, or notify my employer or my ex-husband
that soon, but I felt pressure from my new employer to begin as soon
as possible. What's interesting is that I'd waited several years for God
to bless me, and when he answered my prayer, I wanted Him to slow
down. I was unprepared.

After I accepted the position, I told my ex-husband about the
opportunity, and the conversation did not go well. He disagreed with
the kids moving to southern California despite his inconsistent visits
and lack of involvement. In preparation for taking me to court once I
moved, he wrote me a long email detailing why he disagreed with our
relocation plans and my failure to disclose a possible move.

Added to my stress, I had to break the rental lease I'd just renewed
and was required to pay $3400 to the leasing company. I was also
threatened with a lawsuit by my kids' school because I chose not to

enroll them for the next fall. I wondered, "If this opportunity was from God, then why didn't I receive the job offer one month ago, before I signed my rental agreement and verbally committed to my kids' school for enrollment? What did God want me to learn? Why was His timing off?" But was God's timing off? No. I concluded that God was testing my faith and asking me to trust Him even when things didn't look or go the way I wanted. Rather than worry, I moved forward.

I hired a moving company, left my kids with my parents until I was able to pack up our apartment, and resigned from my job. One of the blessings was that my job kept me on payroll for three more months and paid my personal cell phone bill for six months. I still had to pay the out-of-pocket cost for breaking my leasing agreement, which I later was able to do with the two incomes. Regarding the threat of a lawsuit from my kids' school, I spoke to a lawyer friend, and he agreed to represent me if it went to court if I would help his son with his college essay. I happily agreed. Fortunately, I was never sued, but I was incredibly thankful God placed him in my life during that season.

Several months after I started my new position, I received a call from someone from my office letting me know a strange man wanted to deliver something to me. When I asked her what he left me, she asked me if I'd ever seen the movie *Sweet Home Alabama,* in which the protagonist tries to serve her husband divorce papers. She thought the man wanted to serve me with legal documents. She has asked him to leave the documents with her, promising to personally deliver them to me, but he told her he had to hand-deliver to me himself.

I panicked. The one person who might want to sue me was my ex-husband. I thought he wanted to sue for full custody of our children despite his limited involvement in their lives. I wondered if he was trying to punish me because the court, years before, had granted me alimony and child support.

On a few occasions, my ex-husband had pestered me about having the alimony terminated, but I declined to do so. For three years, my kids and I lived practically hand to mouth while he traveled abroad vacationing. I chose to keep the payments because, by law, I was entitled to receive alimony for a time. It also helped me pay down some of our joint credit card debt. But thinking he wanted to sue me was disturbing. Another thought that came to mind. My kids' school could have decided to pursue legal action against me.

After I stopped letting every negative thought infiltrate my mind, I quietly prayed. Then I called my best friend. She knew I was attending a conference out of town and would return to the office on Monday. She reminded me God is always on my side and that He allowed me to find out I was going to be served before it happened, so I wouldn't be taken by surprise. Your entire outlook on a situation can change depending on your perspective, and once my BFF gave me an alternative perspective, I started to thank God. I appreciated that I had the entire weekend to pray and allow God to minister to my spirit.

I'm sure it sounds strange to be thankful when you're being sued, but I was. I was also thankful no one had been in the office except the person who called me. I was grateful that, when I told my boss what happened, she was incredibly supportive. Everyone else in my life was angry on my behalf, but all I felt was gratefulness.

On Monday, I was prepared. When the man arrived, he gave me the papers, and I opened the envelope. My ex-husband was suing me to terminate alimony and lower what he paid in child support. He was also petitioning the court for us to split the cost of airfare when the kids visited the Bay Area because I chose to leave on short notice and without consulting him. Yet again, I was thankful. I was pleased my ex-husband wasn't suing me for custody. I was relieved his suit was about money, but I was also annoyed.

Part of the reason it took three years for me to pursue a child support and alimony order from the courts was because I was afraid. After my ex-husband left, I didn't want to have an adversarial relationship with him. I wanted an amicable split, so I tiptoed around certain topics, like I did when we were married, to avoid upsetting him. Also, my husband's annual salary, combined with that of his live-in girlfriend, was over $300,000. I was uncertain of my ability to win a custody battle against them.

In that moment, I was afraid of losing custody of my kids. My fear was reminiscent of the story of the twelve spies Moses sent to survey the land promised to the Israelites by God. Ten of the spies returned with a bad report and said, "We can't attack those people! They are stronger than we are" (Numbers 13:31). The people of Israel were afraid to take possession of the Promised Land because they didn't want to face the descendants of Anak. The ten spies said, "We seemed like grasshoppers in our own eyes, and we looked the same to them." (Numbers 13:33). However, two of the spies, Joshua and Caleb, had a different perception. Although they saw the same giants as the other ten spies, they perceived that they were able to conquer giants with God on their side (Numbers 13:30).

The Israelites fought and won many battles against their enemies, but when they came up against giants, they believed they would not be victorious. And despite the number of victories I had won with God, I still cowered at the thought of my husband's resources, as if they were bigger than God.

After I read through the legal brief, I called someone who had helped me in the past on family law matters. I decided to hire an attorney who worked in the Bay Area to cut down on the cost for both of us to fly back and forth. Over the course of six months, I spent over $10,000 on attorney's fees, plane tickets, hotel stays, and taking time off from my new job. Finally, I sat in the courtroom and listened while my ex-husband's attorney painted me as a money-hungry gold digger. He told a courtroom filled with strangers that, even after he left us, he took care of me and our children financially for years. He also told the judge I had a better paying job, and because I wasn't destitute, I didn't need as much money in child support. He further noted that, because he'd paid alimony for two years, it should be terminated.

I was hurt and disappointed by his attorney's depiction of me. The truth was, I didn't want to fight the termination of alimony, but I didn't want child support lowered or to pay to send the kids to visit him. After the judge reviewed the briefs, he ruled to terminate the alimony, lowered the amount I received in child support, and ordered us to split the cost of travel. He also ruled neither of us can ever sue the other over alimony. I was flabbergasted. I could not believe the judge's ruling.

OFFENSE

After I left the court building, I met my best friend for lunch and burst into tears as I shared what happened. She too was surprised by the ruling and expressed frustration. I wanted to know why God allowed him to win. I wondered what lesson I needed to learn from this ordeal. Whatever peace I had was gone. After all the years I'd suffered and tried to do what was right, it didn't seem fair for him to receive everything he wanted. In that moment, it felt like he'd won.

John Bevere, one of my favorite authors, wrote a groundbreaking book called *The Bait of Satan*. He masterfully examined how Satan cleverly lures and baits believers by offense. The introduction of his book starts with, "anyone who has trapped animals knows a trap needs one of two things to be successful. It must be hidden, in the hope that an animal will stumble upon it, and it must be baited to lure the animal into the trap's deadly jaws." He suggests that when believers fall into the deadly trap of offense, they do so without realizing it. He states, "They are oblivious to their condition because they are so focused on the wrong that was done to them. They are in denial. The most effective way for the enemy to blind us is to cause us

153

to focus on ourselves." Well, that was me. I was so focused on the injustice of what happened to me that I couldn't find the blessing.

FINDING THE BLESSING

It took everything in me and all of God's word that I absorbed over the years to not lose myself in disappointment, frustration, and anger. Instead of completely losing my cool and spiraling, I prayed and waited for my peace to return. During prayer, I was reminded of Psalm 37:1-9,

Do not fret because of those who are evil
or be envious of those who do wrong;
for like the grass they will soon wither,
like green plants they will soon die away.
Trust in the LORD and do good;
dwell in the land and enjoy safe pasture.
Take delight in the LORD,
and he will give you the desires of your heart.
Commit your way to the LORD;
trust in him and he will do this:
He will make your righteous reward shine like the dawn,
your vindication like the noonday sun.
Be still before the LORD
and wait patiently for him;
do not fret when people succeed in their ways,
when they carry out their wicked schemes.
Refrain from anger and turn from wrath;
do not fret—it leads only to evil.
For those who are evil will be destroyed,
but those who hope in the LORD will inherit the land.

Through this Psalm, God was telling me not to worry. He saw and knew what was going to happen. He promised to uphold me (Psalm 37:17), not abandon me to the power of the wicked (Psalm 37:33), and be my stronghold during my times of trouble (Psalm 37:39).

Undoubtedly, it was difficult to identify the blessing in the judge's ruling until I quieted my mind. Many women I know must pay alimony and child support to their ex-husbands because those women have climbed the ladder of success. Some are ordered by the courts to pay years after the divorce when their ex-husband experiences financial hardships. Once these thoughts came to mind, I saw God's mercy and blessing. I can only imagine if something were to happen to my ex-husband's finances and he decided to seek alimony from me. Without the court order in place, I could one day find myself in the same position as some of my friends. This was the first blessing I noticed.

Although I didn't want to pay airfare for my children to visit their father, there was fairness in the outcome. Well, that's what I choose to believe. The visitation schedule required I pay for two roundtrip visits per year. If my ex-husband was more active in my kids' lives, I would've had to pay for more than two trips. This was the second blessing I identified.

Just because I am a believer and follow God doesn't mean everything in my life will turn out the way I expect or want. Even when I don't agree or understand the *why*, I know *when* God is for me, who can be against me (Romans 8:31), which He has shown me over and over.

Life Lesson #19
You may feel life is against you at times, but God is always for you, even if you cannot celebrate the truth in the moment.

Finding the blessing in my situation was critical to releasing the offense, which didn't mean I celebrated the outcome, but I remained thankful. I knew whatever I focused on would grow. If I focused on anger, unforgiveness, offense, and resentment, it would metastasize. But when I focused on the goodness of God and His blessings, my mind was at peace. I released the pain and forgave my ex-husband, the judge, my ex-husband's attorney, and my attorney for losing.

Forgiveness means letting go of the offense in your heart and mind. Jesus calls believers to forgive (Luke 6:27-28). So I prayed over the next several weeks that God soften my heart towards all parties and help me to forgive. Each time I prayed the prayer of forgiveness, I let go a piece of the hurt, pain, and offense until it no longer had a hold in my mind and heart.

I no longer saw my ex-husband as the person who robbed me of the life I craved. I saw him as a lost soul, for I knew he did not *know* Jesus. I prayed God would use our divorce to draw my ex-husband closer to Him. And when I prayed for his salvation, I started to feel compassion for someone who wronged me, I and moved towards forgiveness. I used the word *towards* because forgiving someone is difficult. Forgiveness requires spiritual maturity, or in the absence of maturity, trust in His word. I knew God would not lead me astray. I also knew He wanted me to release the thoughts and emotions of hurt, rejection, and abandonment that I felt, which could only happen if I chose to forgive my ex-husband.

> *Key Thought:*
> *Forgiving someone doesn't mean their actions were justified; it simply frees you.*

> *Life Lesson #20*
> *To be completely healed, you must release the offense into God's hands and forgive.*

Sometime after, my ex-husband called, and when I heard his voice, I did not feel anger and hurt, and I no longer felt offense. I smiled on the phone while he spoke. I wondered, "Lord, is this what forgiveness feels like?" I felt an indescribable peace and calm. Scripture states, "I will keep in perfect peace all who trust in you, all whose thoughts are fixed on you" (Isiah 26:3). After trusting God and being obedient to the Holy Spirit, I was delivered from the sting of my husband's decision to take me to court. This is when I met God: The Deliverer and Healer.

Prayer to Forgive

Father, help me to be kind and tenderhearted to the person who offended me. Help me to not repay evil with evil but with blessings. Do not let me give in to feelings of anger, wrath, or the temptation to replay, over and over in my head, how they treated me. Show me how to release the offense in my heart. Lord, your word says if I forgive others for their trespasses, then you will forgive me, but if I do not forgive, then you will not forgive me. Father, I too have made mistakes and hurt others in the past, and you did not withhold your love from me, so grant me the strength I need to move past feeling offended.

In Jesus's name, Amen!

CHAPTER 11
Season of Insecurity and Fear

For the Spirit God gave us does not make us timid, but gives us
power, love and self-discipline.
(2 Timothy 1:7)

IT'S ELEMENTARY

Has God ever called you to do the thing you've struggled with most of your life? Has He asked you to expose a secret or a truth about yourself, to reveal something so personal it's hard to express? Over the years, I've realized God will always ask me to do things outside of my comfort zone, where I generally feel inadequate, insecure, and unqualified. And when He does, the enemy will use my fear to prevent me from moving forward. Whatever my fear or insecurity, it always becomes gigantic in my mind, difficult to fight and overcome.

Most of my adult life, I've wrestled with the belief that my writing was inadequate. During my post-graduate studies, I had a professor who made negative comments on several papers I submitted. When I went to his office hours to discuss his feedback on one of my assignments, he told me that I made too many "elementary mistakes." "This course," he said, "requires strong writing skills." He questioned whether I was ready for the caliber of writing required for the course.

I felt ashamed and embarrassed. I cringed each time I submitted an assignment. Paper after paper, over a sixteen-week period, he continued to make degrading comments about elementary mistakes in my writing. This same professor told the entire class that a few students needed to consider hiring a tutor if we expected to succeed in the class. He said he shouldn't be subjected to correcting grammar. At the moment he made his remarks, his eyes washed over me as if he were announcing to the entire class that he was talking about me. My armpits started sweating because I was certain he would pause and point directly at me.

Over time, my confidence plummeted. The message I rehearsed and played, over and over, in my mind was that my writing was mediocre. It's amazing how something that happened during one season, even on a small scale, caused me to perceive life a certain way. I let the pain of what one person said define how I saw my abilities. I internalized the negative feedback from my instructor and made declarations over myself, such as "My writing is awful" and "not good enough."

For more than twenty years, I carried the emotional scars and lived with the mindset that I made "elementary mistakes" in my writing. Outside of the occasional email, I was apprehensive about writing publicly. If someone asked me to do write-ups, speeches, newsletters, basically anything that required putting my writing skills on display, I avoided it. A more accurate description is that I would say no!

So last year, when God put on my heart to write a book about my journey of coming to *know* Him, I panicked. While I often share my testimony of how I came to know God and the ways He has transformed me during my ten-year walk with friends, family, and at times, complete strangers, I've never had to do so publicly and in writing. Telling me to write about my life experiences and expose my struggles and vulnerabilities was like asking someone who is afraid of heights to go to the rooftop of the tallest building in the world or ride glass elevator overlooking the street to the 80th floor. Just the thought of writing about myself, as someone who suffered occasionally from self-doubt, caused sheer panic. It wasn't the type of panic where I would start to hyperventilate in front of everyone, rather a quiet panic where I instantly felt lightheaded, my eye twitched and lip quivered, the room starts to spin, and my heart raced so fast it felt as if it was going to crash through the cavity wall.

I always have a physical response and panicked reaction when someone asks me to write, especially when I'm asked to write and then read it aloud. My body overheats and my armpits sweat, and heat rises up from my neck, making me feel lightheaded. Once, I had to present something I wrote. I stood in front of a large room filled with people, pulled out my index cards, started reading, and I could have sworn the room started spinning. It felt like I was surrounded by a wall of heat, and I thought I was going to pass out. I wasn't afraid of presenting in front of everyone; I was terrified to read what I'd written aloud.

For most of my life, I've hidden my insecurities about writing, and hiding and pretense went hand in hand. Either I would hide my fears or insecurities or pretend all was well. Over the years, I grew accustomed to concealing parts of myself because it made me feel safe. So exposing something so simple, which many people didn't know about me, felt shameful.

Do you know you can be mentally held hostage by shame? It's a tactic the devil uses to stop believers from being bold and acting with courage. For the record, I don't believe I'm a horrible writer, but that my writing is unexceptional. There are imperfections with the way I write, and because of this, I was, and still am to some degree, concerned that someone, somewhere, will one day make a negative remark for the world to see that says, "Your writing sucks!" More often than not, criticism accompanies writing publicly.

If you ask any of my close friends, they will tell you I prefer staying in the background. In fact, I've described myself as the woman behind the curtain, like the wizard in *The Wizard of Oz*. Not because I consider myself an egotistical, maniacal mastermind or want to control others through fear, but because I like behind-the-scenes roles. I prefer to do the work without taking credit as I orchestrate and implement. This approach doesn't draw much attention. Although many people have described me as an extrovert and someone who loves to openly engage with others, there's a bigger part of me that desires a quiet, peaceful, and anonymous lifestyle. I do not like being at the forefront or on display. And if someone asked me to come from behind my curtain, my fortress of solitude, my answer would be a big fat no!

BABY STEPS TOWARDS PURPOSE

A few years back, a friend and I discussed our difficulty in moving beyond certain fears. We both admitted we were quick in saying no when confronted with something that made us uncomfortable. No, no, no, was our emotional response! This pattern of behavior permeated our lives until we both read Shonda Rhimes's book, *the Year of Yes*. Rhimes, famous for writing hit television shows, such as *Grey's Anatomy* and *How to Get Away with Murder*, describes a fear of speaking publicly that she kept hidden over the years. Her role as a writer and producer were predominantly behind the scenes. However, once her career took off, and she produced more popular television shows, the floodgates opened for speaking opportunities, and she repeatedly said no.

Rhimes recounts a conversation with her sister, who essentially told her that when asked to do something that made her uncomfortable, Rhimes's immediate response was to say no. After some reflection, Rhimes decided that, for an entire year, she was going to say yes to speaking requests, including commencement speeches and talk show appearances. You name it, and she did it. She did it afraid. Her yes helped her confront her deepest fears.

162

After I read Rhimes's book, I asked God to help me confront my fears by saying yes to writing requests. Not long after I prayed about this, a colleague reached out and told me he was receiving an award and asked me to write a quote for the press release. While I had so many wonderful words to share about his achievements, I immediately thought of reasons to tell him no. How ridiculous does that sound? I only needed to write a few words, but I knew whatever words I chose to use would be on display for the world to see. Perhaps that's an exaggeration. Despite my reluctance, I told him yes. This was my first baby step.

Several months later, that same colleague asked me to write an article for a statewide newsletter to encourage educators who were starting off in the counseling field and offer advice on interviewing tips. Again, I contemplated reasons to say no. Although I've worked in K-12 and higher education for more than twenty years and have served on numerous hiring committees, I didn't believe I had any words of wisdom to offer. Doubt and fear crept in my heart, but once again, I reluctantly said yes. This was another small baby step.

Later that day, I told a friend about my colleague's request, and I practically yelled, "Why do people keep asking me to write?" Rather than feel excited, I felt nausea. To say my stress level increased is an understatement. I'm pretty sure my blood pressure skyrocketed as I wondered if I'd make one of those dreaded elementary mistakes for the entire counseling world to see.

That same year, a different colleague asked me to write a research article on school counseling. This time, I did not contemplate saying no. In fact, I enthusiastically said yes. Perhaps saying yes with passion was a way to starve my fears. Although I didn't feel as afraid as I had before, I noticed something else had crept in, which was perfectionism. I became so focused on writing the "right words" that I never wanted to submit the article for publication. Why? Because if the words were not perfect, then I refused to submit it. And there it was again, the belief that my writing wasn't good enough and therefore would invite criticism.

Fortunately, my colleague, who is more of a mentor and friend, told me to (censored word) being perfect. He told me to submit the article and wait for the editors to offer feedback. Over an eighteen-month period, we co-authored four articles together. After my fourth publication was accepted, a close friend asked, "Why don't you write an article alone?" I didn't have the courage to tell her I was apprehensive about submitting an article without having another set of eyes to catch any "elementary mistakes." Instead, I made a lame excuse, which sounded rational at the time.

A few weeks or so passed, and I heard the Lord telling me it was time for me to write my book. I hesitated. It was hard for me to imagine God would ask me to do something that terrified me. But every time I heard a sermon from my favorite YouTube pastors, each one talked about how God was calling some of us to write a book. I heard that same message over and over for several weeks. It was as if God was saying, "Yes. I am aware of your perceived limitations, and I am still calling you to write a book. My power is made strong in your weakness."

What I didn't see at the time was the way in which God used my colleagues' requests, along with others, to gradually tear down insecurities and fearful strongholds in my mind while simultaneously building my confidence. God used my yeses to thrust me towards my purpose, which included writing this book, when He knew fear was standing in the way of His plan. He no longer wanted me to shrink back and run away from something that scared me, but to find my strength, courage, and trust in Him.

Even though I had a knowing in my spirit that God wanted me to write a book, I argued with Him in my head. Have you ever had a one-sided debate with God over something, He's called you to do because you felt unqualified? Well, you're in good company! I am reminded

164

of the story of Moses and how he pleaded with God over his calling and made excuses based on his fears. God told Moses He heard the cries of the children of Israel because of how they were treated by the Egyptians. God told Moses to bring His people out of Egypt, but he panicked. Moses told God, "Who am I that I should go to Pharaoh and bring the Israelites out of Egypt?" (Exodus 3:11). He mentioned to God that he was a shepherd, that no one would believe he was sent or would listen to him, and that he was slow of speech and tongue. But each time, God countered Moses's objection, stating twice that He would be with him. Moses's last plea with God was, "Pardon your servant, Lord. Please send someone else" (Exodus 4:13).

Despite God's assurances that Moses would successfully lead the children of Israel out of Egypt, and they would leave carrying off riches, Moses still didn't want go. Maybe Moses was insecure about being slow of speech and tongue. Perhaps he also knew the Egyptians did not think highly of shepherds and would question his request. What is clear is that Moses preferred to avoid his calling.

Similarly, I did not want to do what God was calling me to do. In fact, I wanted Him to choose someone else. Perhaps if God had laid out for me what I'd encounter and the successes I'd experience like He did with Moses, I would have felt more comfortable moving forward. Well, maybe not. The truth is God was asking me to expose myself. Again, I preferred to live in the shadows, hiding, because my insecurities and flaws are private and not something I wanted on display for the entire world to see.

FEAR GIANTS

Two drivers of my fear prevented me from *quickly* saying yes to writing a book. First, I was afraid I was unqualified to speak on God's behalf, and second, I was scared of making elementary mistakes.

Untrained Spokesperson for God

To share my story about how I came to know Christ, I needed to leverage the Scripture. When talking about the Bible, there are so many opportunities to bend and misinterpret God's word. I'm not a theologian or biblical scholar, and I have never attended seminary school. I'm untrained and unqualified to discuss the historical and religious context of the Bible. I don't know all the books of the Bible and struggle to remember the scriptures. Like many believers, I have unknowingly misinterpreted scriptures. So my insecurities felt valid.

I was afraid someone would criticize my testimony if the scriptures I used were taken out of context. I pictured someone who might write a review saying, "YOU'VE TAKEN GOD'S WORD OUT OF CONTEXT!" My hope and prayer, however, is that God touches hearts, knowing He has placed on my heart the principles I've shared, and the scriptures used to illustrate my testimony whether they're contextually accurate or not.

God qualified me even though I am unqualified. He's using this foolish vessel to share my story about how I came to know Him and the truths that He revealed to me. And while everyone's walk with God will look different, there is a testimony on the inside of you waiting to be poured into this world to glorify His name and be the answer to a problem other need to solve.

Self-Doubt

My other fear that interfered with my immediate yes to my calling was self-doubt. When I think of how God has transformed me over the years, I'm amazed, but I wondered whether other people would be interested in my story. I told myself my personal story would not be revelatory or relevant for anyone. I had so many doubts that prevented me from leaping in faith. Interestingly, I consider myself a natural encourager and a person who has a healthy amount of faith. I love to uplift and motivate other people to step out in faith when they hear from God. But when it came to my personal struggles, I felt trepidation. And because of self-doubt and fear, I started talking myself out of what I *knew* He instructed me to do.

Even when you are living in a delivered state, every now and again, doubt will creep in. You can believe God can do all things, but your doubt can prevent you from believing He can do all things through and with you. I trusted God, but I doubted myself. I believed God could use me, and I saw evidence of Him doing so. My problem was I did not feel worthy to be called by God to do something I was unqualified to do. But I'm thankful for His grace and guidance throughout this entire process.

COURAGEOUSLY CONFRONTING GIANTS

When you are called by God to do something that absolutely terrifies you, it's best to remember that whatever He is asking you to do isn't about you. It's about Him. For weeks, I forgot this. I fixated on my fears and discomfort and not on surrendering, depending, and obeying His voice. I used my timidity and desire to hide as an excuse to not do what I knew God was asking of me.

I was panicked and insecure about the giants who loomed over me. To move forward with God required I courageously confront my perceived mental hurdles, which were my giants. In many ways, David is described in the Bible as a man of courage. Think about how David was anointed to be Israel's next king *before* he encountered Goliath. David *knew* (aware) that God had a greater *purpose* for his life even though it did not immediately come to pass. He trusted God. So when he faced Goliath, a man who stood nine-feet tall, a highly skilled and trained solider who had been in wars since his youth, and likely killed many men, David *remembered* how God protected him in the past (1

Samuel 17:34-36). And just as God delivered him before, He was confident in God, and not himself, that He would do it again.

When people tell the infamous story of David and Goliath, there is so much emphasis on David being a giant killer, that he defeated Goliath with the weapon of Truth on his side, five smooth stones, and a sling shot. And while all of this is true, David defeated Goliath because he trusted in God and it was part of God's plan for his life. David wasn't courageous because he defeated a lion, a bear, Goliath, and his enemies, but because his faith and courage came from God. He trusted that God had a purpose for his life and would bring him victory, not because David was brave, but because he found his worth and courage in Him.

So remember, David knew God (had a relationship), trusted Him (experienced multiple wins with Him), believed God had a purpose for his life, found courage in God (looked back over past victories with God), and fulfilled God's plan and purposes.

Life Lesson #21
Don't confuse courage from God to win your battles with your abilities.

Likewise, God wanted me to draw strength and courage from Him, and not in my ability to say the right words, write perfectly, and quote scriptures. Interestingly, my insecurities and fears of writing were not new but bigger. God revealed I was so focused on the perceived battles ahead (criticisms from others) that I'd forgotten the giants He'd helped me defeat and the many victories I'd experienced. I love how God had a way of showing me, as he showed David, that I'd been there and done that before. Like God did with David, He prompted me to look back over my life. He reminded me that to complete my doctoral program required me to write five chapters, which amounted to more than two hundred pages. My dissertation was reviewed, scrutinized, and approved by more than ten faculty members, who all held PhDs. He helped me remember the feedback I received from the master's dissertation chair, who said, "Vernell, this is one of the best first-round proposals I have had the opportunity to review. It is well written, well-thought-out, well organized, and very thorough."

Similarly, the four academic journal articles I wrote as the primary researcher and writer were peer-reviewed and approved by multiple researchers and published in various counseling journals. One reviewer commented, "This is the best paper I have reviewed in my experience as an editor. The content is useful and very valuable. Great work from start to finish."

Neither my dissertation nor articles were written perfectly. I had to make numerous revisions to my manuscripts, but along the way, I started to believe my writing was finally good enough. I believe God wanted me to alter my perception of my writing and not allow the pain of making "elementary mistakes" decades ago prevent me from walking towards my purpose.

When I sat down to write this book, I realized God never told me what to write about. For three months, I wrestled with uncertainty as I wrote on how God delivered me from a debt mindset. But the more I wrote, the more confusion I felt about how much of my story to tell, whether to incorporate strategies on how to live spiritually debt-free, or what scriptures to use. Friends tried to help me untangle the confusion in my head, but it didn't help. I wanted to obey the voice of the Lord, but I was completely lost and wondered if I'd heard from God clearly.

One day, I was on the phone with my best friend, and she decided to conference in her mother to weigh in on a separate matter we were discussing. When her mother picked up the phone, she was speaking in tongues. When she finished, my best friend told her mother I was on the phone. Immediately, her mother gave me a prophetic word from the Lord. She told me God was calling me to write a book. Wait!

Let's stop right there. Neither I nor my best friend ever told her I'd started writing a book. She even told me the title of my book, which God had revealed to her, and why He wanted me to write on this topic. This wasn't the first time my best friend's mother gave me a prophetic word from the Lord, but it was the confirmation I needed, and it gave me courage.

I listened to all that the Lord told her to tell me. Afterward, I shared my earlier concerns about my desire to remain hidden behind my iron wall of secrecy. My best friend's mother reminded me that Jesus's ministry of healing and repentance was public and not private. He did not hide from the calling on His life. He did not live in the shadows even though He knew He would suffer. He was persecuted, ridiculed, rejected, beaten, and exposed, all to fulfill God's purpose on the earth. And although Jesus didn't want to suffer, He endured for our sake.

Once I was given the title of my book, I was no longer confused about the approach to take. I quickly developed an outline, and since then, there has been a "holy ease" in the writing process.

Life Lesson #22
You can only defeat what you choose to confront.

WALKING IN PURPOSE

God continues to amaze me. He gave me a knowing in my spirit to be an author and confirmed His word. He reminded me when fear stands in the way of what He has instructed me to do, like David, I must look back at the God-led victories as a reminder that He's done it before and will do it again. He has fortified my faith, confidence, and courage in Him, not my ability to write perfectly or draw out biblical principles from reading His word. Therefore, while critics may come, my courage to publish this book rests in knowing it's a part of my purpose.

Awakening to my purpose took years to unfold. I first went through several seasons of trials, tribulations, and afflictions. God waited for me to develop emotionally and spiritually, release unforgiveness, overcome my fears, and learn to fully submit to His will before He revealed my calling and purpose. Without my mind renewal and shifts in my behavior, God would have delayed my calling. God's delay should be seen as a blessing that prevents us from self-sabotaging our calling and purpose.

Just to recap, calling is the assignment given to us by God. He uses our natural abilities or gifts along with our talents to support our God-given assignment. To uncover your calling, you must have a close relationship with God. Through your relationship, and once your desires are aligned with His will for your life, you will understand what He has called you to do. And when the time is right, you'll be awakened to the special thing or things God has purposed you to do. For me, awakening and learning to walk in my purpose has given me an overwhelming sense of confidence that I can truly do all things, including writing, through Christ who strengthens me.

CHAPTER 12
Season of Becoming

Before I was afflicted I went astray, but now I obey your word. You are good, and what you do is good; teach me your decrees (Psalm 119:67-68).

DETOURS

Scripture points out that God has plans for our life, to prosper and not harm us (Jeremiah 29:11). As His masterpiece, He has promised that *His planned purpose* for us shall prevail (Isaiah 14:24). There are no ifs, ands, or buts when it comes to the plans God has for us. But to reach His intended purpose requires unexpected detours that may go against the dreams you have for your life.

Detours are inconvenient, indirect routes that take you down unexpected paths to reach your destination. But a divine detour, according to Tony Evans, is a God-inspired roadblock to take you in another direction. These detours are not meant to prevent you from arriving at your destination but may take you down different path so God can repair and fix something broken or build something in you for the next season He's calling you into. In his book, *Detours*, Evans describes these divine detours as necessary, meant to *positively* interrupt, or in some cases, disrupt our lives to help us *become* who God intended.

God used the disruption to interrupt my life. He didn't cause my ex-husband's unfaithful attitude or tell him to leave me and my children while he started a life with someone else. But He did use it to lead me to my calling and divine purpose. Satan thought the loss of my marriage and my ex-husband's departure would destroy me, and for a while, I thought so too.

This detour was unexpected, not what I imagined, inconvenient, and the most painful experience of my life. I was desperate and broken. My self-worth splintered, and my life seemed to be falling apart. Everything felt barren, like a desolate wasteland. At the time, I couldn't see anything positively divine about being in a broken state, until God stepped in the middle of my mess and stripped me of every self-indulgent, self-reliant, and self-righteous attitude that interfered with His plans for my life, all of which helped birth my ministry. What the devil meant for harm God used for good.

In my pain, He lovingly exposed idols hidden in my heart and wrong mindsets and ungodly behaviors that contradicted His word and will for my life. God prompted me to let go of my marriage, head towards uncertainty, trust Him along the way, navigate through conflict, and part ways with people I loved. He taught me obedience, surrender, and to rely completely on Him.

He reshaped my perspective on marriage, divorce, debt, insecurity, dating, and betrayal. He taught me patience, humility, obedience, surrender, submission, total dependence, and perseverance, and He filled me with His strength. He gave me the boldness and courage to speak and share His word with others. He sharpened my ability to discern His voice and will for my life and overcome many of my fears. He lovingly equipped me for challenges coming and taught me how to pursue peace in all areas of my life even when the storms of life come.

God used my detour to refine, mold, sculpt, and strengthen my character. He helped me mature spiritually, catapulted me towards His divine purpose, and propelled me forward in faith. But there was a price I paid, painful burdens I carried, dreams I had to release, thoughts God had to transform, and periods of uncertainty I had to live through.

RELENTLESS PURSUIT OF GOD'S PURPOSE

Afflictions and the many seasons we find ourselves in awaken, lead, and help us to relentlessly pursue and advance the Kingdom of God. My encounters with Jesus over the years have changed the trajectory of my life and helped me become aware that I was uniquely created to be the solution to a problem that exists. It made me realize He's more interested in my overall development, so I can reach my destiny, than my personal comfort. I've learned the sum total of my life isn't about being successful according to the world's standard, but for me to pursue, prevail, and prosper in His intended purpose.

Everything I've experienced (heartache, betrayal, rejection, fears, and insecurities) and all the individuals I've encountered over the years (friends and haters) were intended to awaken me to my purpose. Nothing in my life is random or happened by coincidence. The predominantly African American environment where I was raised, my socioeconomic background, the college I attended, and the sorority I joined. Also, moving to San Francisco, the law school where I was admitted, the internship I received, friendships I made, and my counseling career helped me to relate to people from different walks of life. These experiences and seasons also took me out of my comfort zone, forced me to grow, and led to the cultivation of my gifts, talents, and calling. They brought greater clarity of my purpose.

Despite the mistakes and challenges I encountered from making the wrong choice in who I married or dated, and the relationships I needed to release, nothing I've experienced has been wasted by God. Every tear I shed, the lessons I learned, and things I questioned about myself were necessary for me to mature spiritually. They thrust me towards God's purpose and who He created me to be. How can I regret my pain if it helped me land where I am today? Because of my disappointments and heartaches, I truly understand what it means to be joyful in hope, patient during affliction, and faithful in prayer (Romans 12:12).

In my afflictions, Jesus taught me what it means to be meek, humble, gentle, and lowly, and stopped me from being arrogant and prideful. He taught me how to forgive and love according to God's word when I'm hurting. He stopped me from being entitled and conceited. He had my children bear witness to the power of a prayer life and what total dependence on God looks like. He helped me see who He created me to be, not the broken me.

Through my suffering, I can better understand and empathize with the afflictions other people endure. My heart and mind are more sensitive to the needs of others. I've become less selfish and strive to focus more on Christ and giving to others and think less about what I want and how I feel. Walking through each season with God on my side has given me a profound appreciation of Psalm 119:71, which says, "It is good for me that I was afflicted, so that I might learn your decrees."

I know Him. I trust Him more. I now know what it means to carry my cross daily and crucify my flesh. Like Job, my ears have heard, but now my spiritual eyes have seen Him. God used my debt, failed relationships, and challenges to strengthen and strip away the old me, the one who was broken, and resurrected the woman of God who is finally whole.

Thank you, Lord, for the gift of interruptions and divine detours, which led me back to You. Thank you for uncertain times and uncomfortable moments, which helped me grow closer and dependent upon You. As my desire to focus on what pleases you increased, you prepared me, took me on unexpected routes, promoted me in faith, and launched me into my calling and purpose. You've given me clarity.

God, you've always had my back no matter the situation or circumstances, and I cannot wait to see all you have in store for me!

CALL TO ACTION FOR BELIEVERS

Go beyond the doors of the church in your quest to know Him more intimately. Run after Him. Chase. Pursue. Submit. Fully Obey. Worship. Unleash. Let him shake you and take you on a divine detour. Get ready for disruption. Prepare to be uncomfortable. Choose His discomfort as you grow and not the world's version of comfort. Chase purpose. Live purpose-driven. Jesus turned this world upside down in three years. Now it's your turn. Choose to know Him.

> ### *Life Lesson #23*
> *You are bigger than the season that you're in.*

ZIGZAG TO PURPOSE

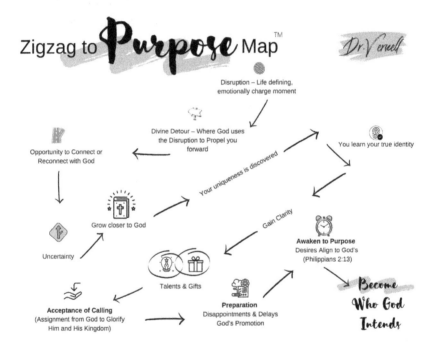

Zigzag to **Purpose** Map ™

Dr. Vernell

Disruption – Life defining, emotionally charge moment

Divine Detour – Where God uses the Disruption to Propel you forward

You learn your true identity

Opportunity to Connect or Reconnect with God

Your uniqueness is discovered

Grow closer to God

Gain Clarity

Uncertainty

Awaken to Purpose
Desires Align to God's
(Philippians 2:13)

Talents & Gifts

Become Who God Intends

Acceptance of Calling
(Assignment from God to Glorify Him and His Kingdom)

Preparation
Disappointments & Delays
God's Promotion

ACKNOWLEDGMENTS

I'd like to thank the countless people who have supported my journey of walking with God and bringing *From Pain to Purpose* to fruition. I've been blessed to be surrounded by a community of men and women who have lifted me and believed in me before I believed in myself. The gratitude that I feel is unexplainable. I'd like to first acknowledge my two beautiful children who unselfishly allowed me to dedicate the time needed to write this book. I could not have done any of this without their support. Thank you also to my parents, Delbra and Theodore Woodard, for your unyielding love, encouragement, and introducing me to Jesus. Thank you to my best friend, Dayshawnna Littleton, for never hesitating to offer on-demand prayers, teaching me how to pray, and leading me into an intimate relationship with God. Your love, guidance, and fighting spirit to always remain faithful to God has been nothing short of inspiring. To my sister, Patrice Sweeney, thank you for your never-ending inspirational words and support over the years to push me to be the best version of myself. And to Charlotte Littleton, a special thank you for showing me what obedience and trust look like in the life of a believer. I would not be the faith-filled person I am without each of you.

ABOUT THE AUTHOR

D R. VERNELL DESLONDE is an acclaimed speaker, Clarity Coach, and devoted mother of two based in Los Angeles, CA. She holds an EdD in Organizational Leadership from Grand Canyon University, Masters degrees in K-12 Counseling and Higher Education from San Jose State University, and a Bachelor's degree from the University of California at Santa Barbara.

You can find out more details about Dr. Vernell at www.drvernell.com